CHINA AND AMERICA
A TIME OF RECKONING

CHINA AND AMERICA

A TIME OF RECKONING

Charles Dumas

PROFILE BOOKS

First published in Great Britain in 2008 by
Profile Books Ltd
3A Exmouth House
Pine Street
London EC1R 0JH
www.profilebooks.com

Typeset in Times by MacGuru Ltd
info@macguru.org.uk
Printed and bound in Britain by
Bell & Bain Ltd

A CIP catalogue record for this book is available from the British Library.

ISBN 978 1 84668 155 4

Contents

Figures and tables

Acknowledgements

This book is a follow-up to *The Bill from the China Shop* of two years ago. Like the earlier book, it owes much to continuing valuable discussion and debate of the global issues with my colleagues at Lombard Street Research, a notable addition to whom in 2007 was our associate Leigh Skene, who has educated us with a crash course in sub-prime derivatives and their dangers. Peter Allen, our managing director, has played a crucial role in keeping the book on track and working on its title and presentation. I am indebted to my partner, Pauline Asquith, for general support and high-quality textual criticism, as with the earlier book.

Introduction

This book's predecessor, *The Bill from the China Shop*, described the limits to the recent boom. Part one of that book forms the Appendix to this book: it is essential to include it. The forecast was that American housing affordability would run out, and that excessive US household debt would stop the global boom that depended on it to finance the importer of last (and first) resort – the American consumer. So it has proved. Denial of the need for a mortgage slowdown in the year to spring 2007 caused Wall Street and its dependent mortgage brokers throughout America to build a disastrous mountain of unserviceable mortgages, which were then retailed around the world in various forms of mortgage-backed securities. The credit crunch which began in 2007 was the result, as the potential $250 billion–300 billion of losses from US mortgage defaults seized up the world's credit and monetary system.

Behind the mounting US debt lay the structural Eurasian savings glut, the causes and effects of which were described in that book (see Appendix, page 99). At that time, the savings glut was $750 billion, with $300 billion each in north-central Europe and Japan/China ($150 billion each for these two) and

$100 billion in the other Asian Tiger economies. The savings glut required equal and opposite borrowers. Nationally, running the corresponding deficits was no problem for the United States (or other big deficit countries such as Britain, Australia and Spain). The problem lay with the domestic borrowing that was the necessary counterpart to the capital inflows. Once housing affordability ran out, as house prices and interest rates rose, the increase in housing collateral was no longer there, nor was the incremental debt capacity to keep the economy on the move.

This book starts with a description of China's soaring economy, its exports and its role in the world economy. China's GDP is over one-tenth of the world's, measured at comparable prices (purchasing-power parity or PPP). Growing at a 10% trend rate, it supplies more than 1% of the 4% trend growth of world GDP (on a PPP basis – it is 3% using market exchange rates and ignoring wide price disparities between developing and developed economies). China's incremental contribution to world output and income is thus huge – and is a third to a half larger than America's. China's role in the savings glut has increased, along with the glut itself. The total has grown by more than a half in two years to $1.2 trillion in 2007, and China's current surplus has more than doubled from $160 billion to $350 billion–400 billion. But this is adding to economic disruption in the rest of the world. China is in danger of serious economic overheating and requires a change of strategy. For the first time since the exchange rate was fixed in 1994, a major yuan appreciation is in China's interests. The risk to China and the world economy is that the Chinese government will not grasp that fact, or at least will do so too late.

Table 1 **Eurasian savings glut: current-account surpluses,**[a]
($bn)

Country/group	2005	2007
Total Eurasian savings glut	765	1,182
of which:		
China	161	361
Japan	166	206
Asian Tigers[b]	100	154
North-central Europe	339	461
of which:		
Germany	128	198
'Inner ring'[c]	211	263

a December 2007 OECD estimates.
b Hong Kong, Indonesia, Malaysia, Philippines, Singapore, South Korea, Taiwan, Thailand
c Austria, Belgium, Denmark, Finland, Luxembourg, Netherlands, Norway, Sweden, Switzerland
Source: OECD

Following on from this the book examines the breakdown of the 2003–07 boom, the end of the 'Goldilocks' economy (see pages 28–9) and the development of the current crisis. It looks at the US mortgage debacle and the likely US economic hard landing. It examines flaws in how central banks have dealt with current global financial problems. It shows how weakness in America could be transmitted to Europe, not by direct trade but by the sharp descent of the dollar – especially if the Chinese yuan clings to its link with the fallen greenback. It outlines the weakness of arguments based on the supposed Asian 'decoupling' from the US economy, likely problems in Britain, Spain and Japan, and the probability of difficulties for the 'resource' economies, whose commodity prices are likely to fall.

For the future, the crucial question is: can any world recovery develop as long as financial imbalances are so marked? The answer is a strictly conditional 'Yes'. The biggest change needed is that the surpluses should flow to deficit countries mostly as equity finance, not – as in 2002–07 – as debt. This in turn depends on Chinese acceptance of active asset management, as far as possible by individuals and businesses rather than the state. It would also be much more effective if recipient countries, primarily the United States, do not fall back on nationalistic controls over foreign ownership in the stockmarket. But that issue in turn would be eased if Chinese capital came from individuals and private-sector firms, not state-controlled funds. And lastly, recovery will depend on avoidance of trade protection in the West in response to aggressive Chinese mercantilism. As this in turn comes back to the yuan exchange-rate issue, primary global economic power clearly lies in Beijing. But with power should come responsibility – for conserving and developing the world economic system as well as China's immediate national interest. Will it?

1

China's expansion out of control

By mid-2007, China's goods exports were running at a $1¼ trillion annual rate (see Figure 1). Their growth rate in 2007 was over 25% compared with the previous year (but less in yuan, which had appreciated 5% over the period). This $1¼ trillion is two-fifths of China's gross domestic product (GDP) of $3 trillion. It was also some 2½% of world GDP, measured at current prices and exchange rates. (On this basis, China's GDP is about 6% of the world's, but adjusted for major price differentials in poorer countries compared with rich ones – that is, adjusting GDP to PPP – it is over 10%.) The effect of the new, huge size of these exports combined with their explosive growth dominates the world economy.

The annual growth of China's exports alone is ½–¾% of world GDP: with the latter at $53 trillion, its 3% trend growth rate amounts to an annual increment of $1.5 trillion–1.6 trillion. China's exports of $1¼ trillion growing at over 25% per year (see Figure 2) are adding more than an annual $300 billion, one-fifth of total world growth and 0.6% of world GDP itself. This is a massive displacement of existing supply chains. It is conventional

Figure 1 **China's trade**
US$bn per month, seasonally adjusted by Lombard Street Research

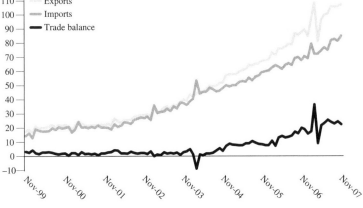

Source: General Administration of Customs

to look at net exports (exports minus imports) in assessing such effects. Goods imports are three-quarters of exports, and growing at 20% (in dollars), well below export growth. All this means that the annual increase in imports is running at about $180 billion, between a half and three-fifths of the dollar value of export growth. So the annual growth of net exports is $120 billion, by itself ¼% of world GDP.

The displacement in the rest of the world resulting from this dynamic Chinese foreign-trade growth must be related partly to the gross and partly to the net export change. Many of the imports come from countries that are not particularly affected by the displacement effect of China's export growth: the Middle East as a source of oil, for example, or Australia as a source of coal and

Figure 2 **China's trade growth**
6 months on 6 months; seasonally adjusted annual rate, %

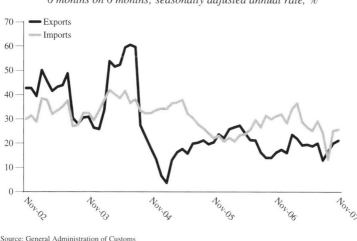

Source: General Administration of Customs

iron ore. (It is right to observe that these countries will themselves spend some of their extra income on industrial country goods and services, but, as will become clear, Chinese demand is crucial to the price upswing of these resources, which has had an additional net negative income effect on western economies.)

North America and Europe take roughly one-fifth each of China's exports. Its imports from both are small. Its low-cost supply has positive effects in cost terms. But its demand effects can be damaging:

• If it is domestic production being displaced, real incomes may be lowered: this will be affected by the ease of shifting resources to higher value industries in the United States and Europe

7

- The relative inefficiency of Chinese production in its use of energy and raw materials means the global price of these is being raised by the displacement of non-Chinese producers by cheap Chinese labour (see page 75). This will reduce real incomes and spending power in other countries.

Other things being equal, fiscal or monetary policy may need to be eased to offset the China effect. What has happened 'on the ground' is that the Asian saving glut – of which China's huge and rapidly growing surplus is now the most important part – has provided from 2003 to early 2007 a major monetary stimulus, through the flow of liquidity and the depression of interest rates and credit spreads – which have been below what would normally prevail at current levels of economic activity. Easy money has been achieved with central banks largely in a supporting role. This stimulus has involved the conventional interplay of greed and fear that dominates financial market cycles, with the latter allayed. But the ease of achieving low inflation has flattered monetary policy and contributed to bubble-type risks – storing up future trouble through over-inflation of asset prices rather than the conventional inflation of goods and services prices (see page 28). And it is important to note that the Chinese (net) export displacement effect has become rapidly larger. So the potential disturbance from large and rapidly growing Chinese trade has to be absorbed by financial markets that are already traumatised by the consequences of recycling lesser Eurasian surpluses in 2003–07.

China's boom has had obvious benefits for its commodity

suppliers in such places as Australia and the Middle East, but the import side of the story partly reinforces the displacement effect. China's GDP in PPP is over 10% of the world total. Its manufacturing measured at current prices and exchange rates is a little under 3% of world GDP. Adjustment to industrial country prices would take that up to about 4% of world GDP at PPP, two-fifths of its total GDP. This high ratio reflects China's industrial-intensive development, led by manufactured goods exports. (These are 'ballpark' figures, not precise estimates.) On the same ballpark basis, if world manufacturing is a quarter of world GDP, China is doing one-sixth of the world's manufacturing in value terms. As it is concentrated at the end-process, assembly end – taking parts made abroad and putting them together – its share of global assembly has to be dominant to the point of monopoly. Further progress in manufacturing remains a priority, bearing in mind the materialistic, mercantilist bias of the Chinese government's thinking and policy. But this must now largely come from moving back upstream – making the parts for assembly.

Manufacturing parts is generally more sophisticated than assembly as it involves greater labour skills. (Whether it is more or less capital intensive is irrelevant in a country with a surfeit of savings.) The parts currently imported by China generally come from nearby powerhouses Japan, South Korea and Taiwan. The slow growth of imports implies that import substitution is taking place on a significant scale, resuming the hollowing-out of these countries. While nominal GDP grew at about 16% in 2007, in dollar terms that is 21–22%. With exports growing at 27%, the under-20% growth of imports takes some explaining. Normally, import growth would come in somewhere between GDP and exports, that is, at around 25%. In economic boom-times it is common for import growth to exceed that of both domestic demand and exports, implying it might be expected to be over 25% in China's case in 2007.

It may be that imports are being paid for and registered late – to delay relinquishing yuan for currency – and exports early – to accelerate turning the currency into yuan. This distortion, known as 'leads and lags', was common in the fixed-currency era whenever major exchange-rate adjustments were expected. But the strong statistical evidence supports anecdotal claims of import substitution as a chief cause of slow Chinese import growth. This means the global displacement arising from the Chinese trade explosion is that much larger.

Commentators have tried to downplay the significance of Chinese exports to growth by observing that a large proportion of exports represents re-export of imported parts assembled into final products. It is claimed that export industry value-added is only 10% of GDP, and that this is the true measure of the export ratio in the economy – not too different from the US and Japanese ratios. But this is a fallacy. Gross exports are 40% of GDP; gross imports are 30%. If the true contribution of exports was only 10%, the entirety of those imports would have to be incorporated in exports to reduce the gross 40% ratio to 10%. In other words, not one single import could be for the satisfaction of domestic demand. This is patent nonsense. High ratios of imports for re-export are common in entrepôt economies like Hong Kong, or even the Netherlands and Belgium, and quite high ratios have been the case in China. But those days are going. Import substitution is the process by which (among other things) China's domestic value-added ratio in exports is being steadily raised.

Mounting surplus and domestic overheating

Two immediate effects of these export and import trends are an exploding overseas surplus and serious domestic overheating. Exports and imports roughly matched one another until 2004 – and the domestic private investment boom that blew itself out in the first half of that year even pulled imports slightly ahead for a few months. For the full year, the current account surplus was $70 billion. But since then, consistently slower growth in imports than in exports, which have maintained an average 30% growth pulse, has meant the current surplus mounting to $170 billion in 2005, $250 billion in 2006 and $350 billion–400 billion in 2007.

The Bill from the China Shop, written towards the end of 2005 (two years ago), estimated China's current surpluses of $180–212 billion in 2006 and $216–296 billion in 2007 (after a then-expected $150 billion in 2005). China's surplus has easily exceeded those forecasts. This mounting surplus is by itself ensuring that the Asian element of the Eurasian savings glut is soaring, raising all the time the required borrowing in deficit countries to offset it. On reasonable assumptions, and with little change in basic economic policy, the surplus could rise in the years to 2010 to the $650–930 billion range. The rest of the world will not be able to borrow enough to handle this. China's exports by

2010 are likely to have risen from 2.5% of world GDP to 4%. Continued expansion on the current scale seems certain to pop the rivets somewhere – unless the very nature of the capital flows is changed (see page 86).

In theory, an overseas surplus taken into foreign-exchange reserves can be sterilised from causing domestic monetary stimulation by financing the extra reserves with bond sales to the non-bank private sector. In practice this has not happened in China. In Germany, where it was achieved in the 1960s, sterilisation became less and less feasible as the government ran out of bond issue requirement – budget surpluses were needed to offset the inflationary impact of the growing trade surplus. Faced with inevitable inflation at the fixed exchange rate, the Bundesbank gave way and the long upward march of the Deutschmark began. China is much less well placed to sterilise than Germany was then. It does not have a free-market banking system, and the prevailing level of government bond yields – 4%, 3% below inflation – is hardly going to induce savers to rush in with their hard-earned cash. The result? Broad money growth consistently in the 16–18% region. Given a trend growth rate just below 10%, it was always likely to be only a matter of time before GDP overheated and inflation caused nominal GDP growth to close the gap (see Figure 3).

Domestic overheating – so long as anything like current trends continues – will mean the Chinese government can no longer ignore the exploding surplus. In yuan terms, exports are growing at 20%, imports at 15%. The difference between these two growth rates applied to the respective numbers means that the increase in net exports (that is, in the trade surplus) has by itself been

Figure 3 **China shifts into overheating**
%

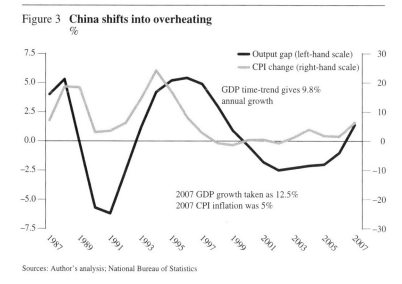

Sources: Author's analysis; National Bureau of Statistics

3–4% of GDP, though this has lessened during 2007. But nominal domestic demand has recently been growing at 17%. Although consumer price inflation has risen to 6½–7%, this is all accounted for by food prices – manufactured goods prices are hardly moving up at all (yet), so that the half of domestic demand that is not consumer spending has little price inflation in it. This means that the inflation number for domestic demand is unlikely to be over 4%. Deducting this from 17% nominal domestic demand growth, its real (price-adjusted) growth is over 12%. With trend GDP growth (the longer-term 'speed limit') under 10% and net exports still adding to growth on top of domestic demand, this is dangerously inflationary.

China's real GDP growth between the early 1980s and today

has on average been 9.8% (based on the growth inherent in a fitted time-trend) and there seems little reason to think it has changed much in recent years. With the current increase of net exports, real domestic demand growth would have to be cut to 7–8% to keep GDP growing at its trend rate – and avoid overheating and inflation. But total domestic incomes are growing in parallel with GDP – their real rate would be 9.7% if GDP could be restrained to 9.7% growth. This means that people would have to save an ever higher proportion of their income to keep domestic demand down to 7–8% growth. Yet China's national savings rate (its GDP minus consumer spending and government current spending) is already a staggering 50% – one of the highest ever recorded. To increase this further by an increased net export contribution each year would be madness. It is also probably unachievable.

Returning to the real world, China's national savings rate is indeed increasing – that is what the rising net export surplus implies, unless capital spending were falling as a share of domestic demand. With real GDP increasing possibly as fast as 13%, and domestic incomes in parallel with that, it is little surprise that real domestic spending is moving ahead at 12%. After all, China's inhabitants are mostly not very rich, and are already saving a large proportion of their income – so why would not export industry workers, for example, spend a large part of their rapidly rising wages? That seems to be what they are doing. As a result, real GDP growth could easily accelerate until at least the growth of imports rises to match that of exports and eliminates the net export contribution to growth. But that probably implies real GDP growth in the mid-teens or even higher. Not only is current real growth of up to 13% leading to overheating, but the overheating will worsen rapidly even if growth merely continues at the present rate – and it could easily accelerate.

The problem of inflation

Why has there been no explosion of inflation yet? The answer probably lies in the scale of the slack that arose in the economy as a result of the Asian crisis in 1997–99, and then the synchronised world downswing in 2001–02. When a time-trend is fitted to China's real GDP since the early 1980s (producing the 9.7% growth trend referred to above), GDP is seen to have been below that trend from 2001 to 2006 (Figure 3). This means that the economy has had slack in it for six years. Only now, with output above trend, is it overheating. But previous periods of overheating suggest that the inflation rate responds by moving quickly upwards, once overheating starts. The rapid acceleration of inflation in China in 2007 (see Figure 4) has somewhat pre-empted this, being entirely confined to food prices and partly caused by pig disease. With real growth probably 13%, and recently accelerating, the government has a huge problem – and can almost certainly not wait until after the 2008 Olympic Games to act.

Inflation could spread to goods prices during 2008, and the overall rate could move towards double figures as the Olympics approach. The presumption has always been that generating jobs is the most important way for the communist government to ease social tensions. But accelerating inflation could create trouble in

Figure 4 **China's consumer price inflation**
    % change year on year

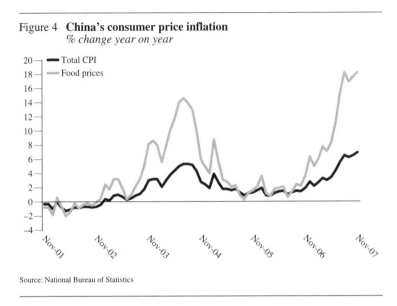

Source: National Bureau of Statistics

two ways. The first is the obvious instability, with certain groups left behind, though so far the concentration of inflation on food prices has redistributed income to rural areas – a policy goal of the government anyhow. The second is that the bulk of Chinese household savings are lodged with state-owned banks at interest rates some 3% below inflation. As the latter accelerates the erosion of existing savings would probably worsen, forcing additional saving merely to hold up the value of existing assets. In a country with little general social security, and relatively undeveloped private financial systems – pensions, health insurance, mortgages, and the like – the sight of hard-earned savings being devalued by growing inflation could cause serious problems.

China's government is facing a 'trilemma' of options:

- **Accept inflation.** This almost certainly means it will accelerate from the current 6½–7%. Aside from the disruption of inflation, it could stoke the credit boom and the flight from money, the real yield from which could worsen from –3%, with a political backlash.
- **Deflate domestic demand.** This is both painful and arguably unnecessary. The need for it is heightened by the low yuan leading to imported cost inflation, and continued gains of net exports that ensure a superfluity of total demand as well as excessive income growth.
- **Let the yuan appreciate radically.** This would directly cut prices of many important imports (including food) and address the unnecessary growth of net exports, which is currently swelling an already huge surplus.

The correct answer is obvious: net exports are already huge and causing China significant problems in the rest of the world. Reasonable prudence requires no further accumulation of reserves. So domestic demand should be allowed to rise with incomes at roughly 10% and net exports stabilised or reduced by yuan appreciation to check inflation. Note the word 'net'. Exports and imports probably will continue to grow faster than GDP, whose own nominal growth has been over 20% recently in dollar terms (17% in yuan). And imports need to rise faster than exports in percentage terms, as they advance from a lower base.

The problem with this obviously optimal policy is simple: the controlled, undervalued yuan exchange rate has been a cornerstone of China's mercantilist development strategy. While that strategy may not have been perfect, the results have been impressive: nobody could call policy to date a failure. So it is unlikely that the theoretical logic of major yuan appreciation will be accepted until the pain of the alternatives has been allowed to intensify enough to induce some risk-taking. (China's leaders are said to be obsessed with the Japanese 'mistake' of letting the yen rise fast in 1985–95. But few others would put that among Japan's major errors, and many would say that a more rapid rise of the yen in the earlier phase, the late-1980s, might have helped cool the bubble.)

The course of affairs until after the Olympics seems set. The shift of exports and export growth to Europe from the United States could keep the surplus growing at least until spring 2008. Some half-hearted tightening of domestic policy may be attempted, but not enough to prevent real domestic demand growth above the 10% long-term trend of GDP growth. Add in net export growth and GDP itself will be growing significantly faster than 10%. Inflation could soon start to become alarming.

One important palliative measure being mooted by some government agencies right now is the removal of controls on capital exports by individual Chinese. It has numerous advantages over the rational alternative: national asset allocation within a sovereign investment fund. (The policy to date of accumulating reserves and shoving them out into dollar money markets at low interest rates in a weak currency is ludicrously docile. Moreover, it depends on the US appetite for extra debt, which has almost certainly been lost for the time being, given the recent crisis – see page 35.)

China's economy in fundamental disequilibrium

Pending the adoption of such measures, much enhanced freedom to export capital and a major rise in the yuan's exchange rate, China's economy is essentially out of control, in fundamental disequilibrium. The inherent conflict between a desire both to prevent inflation and to sustain an artificially low, semi-fixed exchange rate is not being addressed, and cannot be removed without either painful and unnecessary domestic deflation, or abandoning the shibboleth of the undervalued yuan–dollar rate. The current policy stance can probably just be sustained until after the 2008 Olympics, but the pressures will mount – especially from angry Europeans whose artificially high exchange rates are the chief current indicators of China's policy distortion.

Whereas in 2006 the growth of China's exports to the United States and Europe was about the same (although their value was greater to the United States), in 2007 export growth to the European Union accelerated to 36% while that to the United States decelerated to 15% (see Figure 5). As a result, China's exports to the European Union now exceed those to the United States and are mounting faster. The growth alone of China's exports to the European Union in 2007 will amount to 3% of China's GDP – with very little taken back in imports. With Europe now its largest and fastest-growing market – and unrelenting US pressure to let the yuan appreciate against the dollar – a rising euro is strongly in China's interest. To be sure, this is inefficient in terms of China as an investor (of its reserves, which are mostly in dollars). But it means the yuan can appreciate at 5% vis-à-vis the dollar and yet depreciate against the

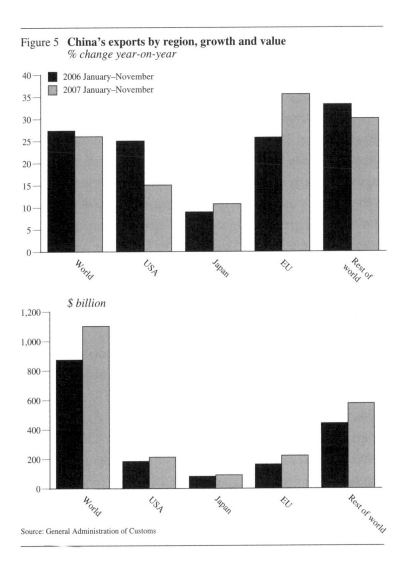

Figure 5 **China's exports by region, growth and value**
% change year-on-year

Source: General Administration of Customs

euro, which is gaining more, making mercantilist exporter China
even more cost-competitive in Europe than before.

While the United States encourages devaluation of the dollar (see page 54), China's $1½ trillion of reserves are a powerful weapon with the same goal. Against them is ranged a euro zone that does not even have a mechanism for forming an exchange-rate policy – let alone such a policy itself. But before analysing Europe's problems, it is worth looking at how the forecasts of a US slowdown in *The Bill from the China Shop* have played out – where they have been vindicated, and where not.

2

Overborrowed America

One basic weakness of global imbalances as engines of growth in 2002–06 was the asymmetry between saving and borrowing. Eurasian savings-glut countries (see pages 117–29) save to build up assets. This can be done without obvious limit. The counterpart borrowing countries – more particularly the domestic borrowers within them – kept the world economy moving by living beyond their means, the growth in their debt made possible by rapid asset-price growth as capital flowed in from the savings-glut countries (see Figure 6). The asymmetry is clear: debt, unlike assets, cannot be run up faster than income indefinitely.

The Eurasian savings glut had expressed itself in equity capital flows to the United States and other deficit countries in 1998–2000, but that stopped when the bubble burst. In 2002–07, capital flows from surplus to deficit countries within Europe have been largely in the form of debt rather than equity. And the 'main course' – the trans-Pacific flow of the Asian savings glut to the United States – mostly took the form of a build-up of foreign-exchange reserves in Pacific Rim countries which was entirely concentrated on debt instruments. The nature of the

Figure 6 **US domestic debt**
% of GDP

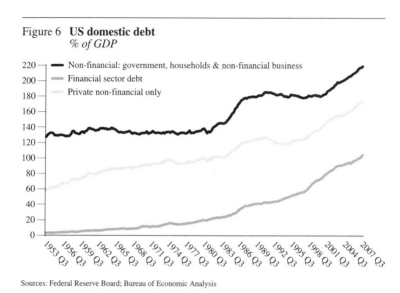

Sources: Federal Reserve Board; Bureau of Economic Analysis

'New Dollar Area' and the fundamentals of the Asian savings glut and its absorption by US borrowing are described in the Appendix.

The point of the Eurasian savings-glut thesis in its original form in 2004–05 was that America's external deficits were not (and are not) a problem. They are essential to the excess savers as an outlet for their investment needs. But the internal run-up of debt in deficit countries would soon become a problem – and the expected location of that excess debt problem was US household mortgages (see Figure 3 in the Appendix). This has proved right.

An important part of the argument is that total flows in the economy add up to zero: for every lender there has to be a borrower, and vice versa. The US deficit with foreigners can be restated as foreigners being in surplus. It follows that the combined domestic sectors of the US economy, household, business and government, had to be running a deficit equal to this foreigners' surplus: at its peak (late 2005 and 2006) some 6½% of GDP, over $800 billion. However, the business sector, badly burned by the experience of 2000–02 as the bubble burst, was still running a surplus of 2% of GDP – depreciation plus retained profit exceeding capital spending. This meant the deficit that had to be absorbed by the combined borrowing 'efforts' of the household sector and the government was 8½% of GDP. While the economic recovery in the United States was kick-started by tax cuts in 2001 and 2003, showing up as extra government borrowing, more than the

Figure 7 **US financial flows**
% of GDP

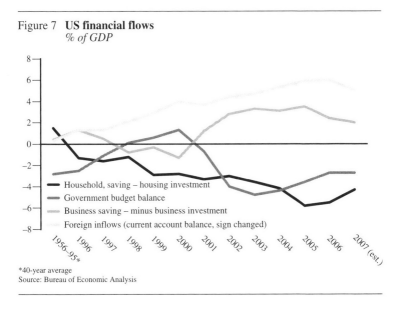

*40-year average
Source: Bureau of Economic Analysis

entirety of debt growth in the economy after that, relative to GDP, was in households: the government deficit soon started to move back downward (see Figure 7).

This liquidity-driven expansion, induced by the savings glut, was always self-limiting. It depended on a continuous rise in debt relative to income, illustrated in Figure 6 (for the United States). How this limit is reached can be described as follows:

- Growing Asian surpluses are offset by US current deficits which rose to 6½% of GDP by 2005–06. These deficits are exactly equivalent to saying that domestic demand exceeded output (GDP) by 6½%. As total domestic income equals GDP, this means that US domestic demand is 106½% of domestic income. In other words, the nation is overspending its income by 6½% (see Figure 8). To finance this, it is borrowing from world financial markets, themselves funded by savings-glut countries.

- To achieve growth in GDP at its 3% trend rate therefore requires much more borrowing to finance the 6½% of extra demand compared with income, on top of the conventional increase of debt associated with growth.

- Stable growth at the trend rate thus involves a continuous and unstable rise in the ratio of debt to income. Likewise, to provide collateral for this indefinite increase in debt, asset prices needed to rise faster than incomes – in effect for ever.

- At some stage limits on the service of this growing debt must prevent extra borrowing and therefore ensure below-trend demand (and thus income) growth.

- Slowing income aggravates the overhang in householders' balance

Figure 8 **US household debt measures**
% of disposable income

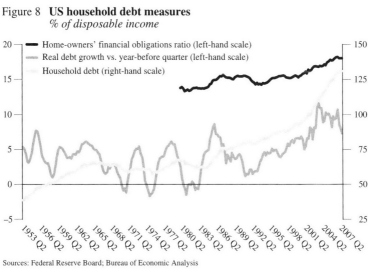

Sources: Federal Reserve Board; Bureau of Economic Analysis

sheets of excess debt, and the economy risks descent into a deflationary tail-spin.

The negative effects of the last two points started in the spring
of 2006, when US house prices had been static to slightly declining for about half a year (see Figure 9). Until spring 2007 they
were largely confined to the housing and real estate businesses:
soaring house prices and rapidly rising interest rates had ham-
mered affordability, and therefore demand for new and existing
homes. The effects of continued house-price slippage usually
spread by a 'slow-burn' process (higher savings rates) to the rest
of the economy – with growing nervousness about the burden
of the household debt build-up as house-price collateral erodes.

Figure 9 **US housing: home prices**

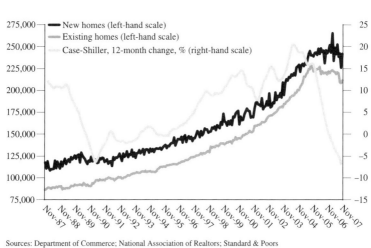

Sources: Department of Commerce; National Association of Realtors; Standard & Poors

What was surprising was the extent to which the mechanics of the mortgage debt explosion would continue to operate, in some sort of flywheel effect. As a result, huge swaths of entirely unrepayable mortgage debt would be added during 2006 and early 2007 to the already excessive levels at the end of 2005.

The 'Goldilocks economy' has broken down, but what was it based on?

- **Globalisation.** The shift of manufacturing to cheap-labour countries, mostly Asian, notably China, lowered goods prices.
- **Offsetting/using up the savings glut.** People in deficit countries were called upon to enjoy themselves spending more than their income – for the sake of the nation.

- **Savings glut led to capital flows and liquidity.** Meanwhile, despite overspending, they got wealthier as the savings glut flowed into asset prices, extra wealth (especially housing) serving as collateral for the increased debt involved in overspending incomes

- **Globalisation again.** The explosion of financial activity based on savings-glut liquidity created a huge flow of income in countries (notably the United States and the UK) with sophisticated financial systems – which also happened to have much of the offsetting deficits.

These four elements have gone wrong in roughly that order.

- Developing Asia may pay low wages, but it is high-cost in resource usage, being much less efficient than high-income countries in the use of energy, metals, and so on. As Asian growth rates have been high, this waste has pushed up the cost of resources, hitting hardest the United States, with its energy dependence greater than Europe and Japan, and its currency weak. As world growth is healthy, these extra costs have helped revive inflation.

- Central banks, especially the Federal Reserve in the United States, started to raise interest rates. This interacted with higher prices of assets, especially houses, to cut housing affordability just as over-investment was kicking in. This meant the days of 'borrow-and-spend' became numbered. The fatal flaw of the Goldilocks economy was its dependence on ever-rising debt ratios in deficit countries.

- The frenzied denial by financial markets of the need for any kind of 'landing' – at least as regards their own activities and incomes – caused those involved with financial markets to develop huge

appetites for risk just as the reward for risk in the form of extra yield
was shrinking. In traditional boom–bust fashion, this has now collapsed 'under its own weight'.

The accelerating liquidity of the year and a half to mid-2007
was concentrated in two areas: unsound mortgages and the use by
businesses of debt finance to buy back equity, mostly in the form
of private-equity leveraged buy-outs. The mechanism by which
this has been driven has been compression of lending 'spreads'
– the differentials in borrowing cost arising from differences in
credit quality. For example, the extra yield available to investors
in 'junk' (low-quality) bonds averaged about 5% in 1990–2003,
compared with ten-year US government bonds (Treasuries); by

Figure 10 **Junk spreads rising**
KDP index minus 10-year Treasuries, percentage points

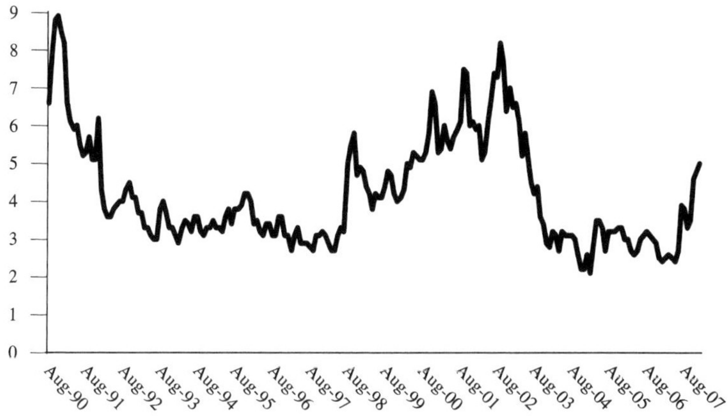

Sources: KDP; Federal Reserve Board

early 2004 this differential had fallen to 3%, staying around that level until 2006 before falling to 2½% in the first half of 2007 (see Figure 10). Reinforcing the cuts in Treasury yields themselves in 2003–06, this compression was inherently self-limiting: at the very least spreads can hardly fall below zero.

The question became: which would be the weakest link in the credit chain to snap first? The answer turned out (unsurprisingly) to be the area of greatest excess in the previous boom: low-end, 'sub-prime' mortgages in the United States. Serious problems are also emerging in Britain and Spain, as well as in other smaller economies where growth has been chiefly driven by a house-price and mortgage boom. All mortgage activity and outstanding debt is affected, of course, and contagion has extended to corporate debt, temporarily halting the private-equity business in its tracks: bank loans for all new purposes have dried up, and the junk bond spread (see above) has risen from 2½% to over 5%.

US housing: the boom loses its affordability

Housing affordability is a mix of three factors. Houses become more affordable with increases in incomes, lower house prices and lower interest rates. The natural measure of affordability is to find out what the monthly (or annual) cost of a 25- or 30-year mortgage is on 100% of the value of the median-priced house in any country – and then show that as a percentage of the median household income. If it is going down, houses are reducing their all-in cost relative to income, so affordability is going up.

And vice versa all the way through the last three sentences. US incomes were quite buoyant from mid-2003 onwards, assisted by tax cuts. House prices were rising faster, but not much faster. The chief damage to affordability as 2004–05 wore on arose from the end of the ultra-low interest rates of 2002–03. Shifts in interest rates have generally caused the biggest variations (up and down) in housing affordability: for example, at interest rates of around 5–6%, a 1% change in the interest rate affects mortgage affordability as much as an 11% change in the house price.

US housing affordability started to lose ground in the spring of 2004, when the rise in prices hit its peak of 20% (see Figure 11). From June 2004, the Federal Reserve started to put up interest rates. No longer was the US economy flat on its back, in danger of deflation. Inflationary risks had been further winched up by rapid escalation of oil and metal prices. As a measure of US housing affordability, the cost of mortgaging the entire US housing stock at current prices over 30 years can be calculated as a percentage of total disposable income, using both the 30-year fixed rate and the 1-year adjustable rate. (In affordability charts the scale is inverted to reflect lesser affordability when a larger proportion of income is required to service the mortgage.) From the first quarter of 2004 to the second quarter of 2006, the percentage required moved for the fixed-rate option from 12.8% to 16.3%, an increase of over one-quarter; and for the adjustable-rate option from 10.1% to 14.7%, an increase of nearly a half.

Although adjustable-rate mortgage costs increased faster than those for fixed-rate mortgages, adjustable rates remained less costly. Not surprisingly, as the going got tougher, borrowers

Figure 11 **US and UK housing affordability indices**

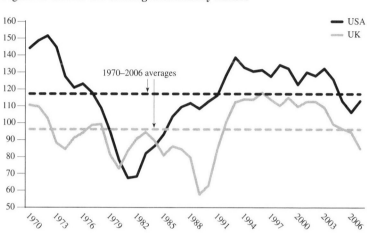

Sources: National Association of Realtors (US); Lombard Street Research (UK)

turned to them more. What was surprising was that the chairman of the Fed, Alan Greenspan, encouraged borrowers to move to adjustable rates – to increase affordability. With short-term rates going up as part of Fed policy, both before and after he made this recommendation, it was at the very least a lure towards the Faustian bargains that were increasingly being offered – 'teaser' mortgages, with very low initial payments.

The idea of a teaser mortgage rate was simple. Suppose the quality of loans declines as household debts rise relative to house prices and incomes, while the new entrants to the market are further down the income scale. Then how about offering an 8% loan, but with payment at only 3% of the principal for two years? The 8% already reflects an inferior quality loan. (Mortgage rates

33

in 2006–07 for regular quality borrowers were 6–6½% for fixed and 5–5½% for adjustable.) Because the payment for two years is 5% shy of the interest rate, the amount owed after two years has gone up to (roughly) 110% of the original principal. The resulting payment – for the 28 years remaining of a 30-year mortgage, for example – would be 10% of the original principal amount (including normal amortisation in a repayment mortgage). If the repayment schedule had been started at the signing date for the full 30 years, the monthly payment would have been only 8.9%.

For a typical American mortgage of $200,000, the payment, which would have been $1,480 a month on a regular 30-year repayment basis, was lowered to $333 a month for two years, but then 'reset' to $1,660 a month. By early 2007, the sub-prime borrowers' repayment capability had gone down to such a degree that the true rate being offered was often in double figures, for example an 11% loan on which the first two years' payments were made at 'only' 7%. By this stage the mortgage 'sausage machine' was dealing in very little true meat at all – and the wilful suspension of disbelief in the financial markets that turned such loans into the basis for triple-A rated loans (see next section) was taken to the intensity previously seen in financial market manias. The worsening of affordability reached the stage of stopping the rise in house prices actually transacted by September–October 2005. The most comprehensive measure of US house prices levelled off then, but managed another 2% increase before its peak in June 2006. Within six months of the end of price gains in new home sales in autumn 2005, builders realised that the game was up. The house-building collapse started in spring 2006. What should also have started then was a sharp slowing of mortgage lending, and of the household spending based on it. Instead of that the Wall Street sausage machine, pulling together the efforts of deal-hungry mortgage brokers countrywide, carried on churning out 'sausages' with less and less meat: that is, means of repayment. Thus was what could have been a relatively benign economic and financial slowdown transformed into a credit crunch and liquidity crisis.

The banks lay off the loans: the US sub-prime fiasco

'Cometh the hour, cometh the man' – or in this case, the means. 'You got a dream? – Here's the money!'

How much money can a person afford to borrow? How much debt in aggregate can US households afford relative to their income? Obviously, the lower the interest rate the more debt can be serviced. But suppose US inflation is expected to average 2–2½%. And suppose the days of artificially low real interest rates, courtesy of the savings glut, are gone. Then the future trend of interest rates can only be seriously downward if the economy has got into trouble. That would hardly be the moment to ramp up debt. In other words, the scale of debt that has rendered housing at the limit of affordability at recent mortgage rates is a natural upper limit. Since autumn 2005 American house prices have been static to declining. Yet confronted with the clear need to scale back the growth of borrowing, Wall Street went for magic potions instead: an extravagant expansion of multi-layered asset-backed securities to make a silk purse out of a sow's ear, to transform lead into gold.

The basic concepts are simple to understand. In the old days a bank would lend money for house purchase via a mortgage – for example, with a 25-year repayment schedule. This involved some risk of the mortgage-taker defaulting at some stage over the 25 years. Suppose the bank took the same risk vis-à-vis a large number of householders. Provided they were roughly similar in character-istics (for example, income, house price), these loans would default at about the average rate for such loans. Suppose 1% was the long-run average rate of loss from defaults. Then the bank would need to charge householders 1% more than its own cost of funds to justify the risk – plus a further margin, say 0.5%, to cover risk: that is, secure a good return on the equity base or reserves it would need to have in place to insure against the default experience turning out worse than normal. Suppose the bank was not rated AAA (the top rate – few are) but perhaps single-A. (In between comes double-A, traditionally a pretty low degree of risk.) Then the mortgage inter-est cost to the householders would be the single-A rate for 25 years plus rather over 1%: 1.5% in this example.

The idea of a mortgage-backed security is to remove the bank from this credit chain – to cut out the middleman. By the end of the 1980s, the previous debt-fuelled American boom had burned itself out and added major domestic bad-debt problems to the banks' left-over wrecked assets resulting from the earlier Latin American overlending. By general consent, Citibank (for example), had it been wound up in 1990, would have proved insolvent. A Citibank bond issue might cost it significantly more than the single-A rate; together with its own on-lending margin in making a mortgage loan this would add up to a major burden on household borrowers. But banks like Citibank, the largest in America, do not like to be cut out of the mortgage business. The solution was to find a way of making mortgage advances that did not involve the interpolation of Citibank itself into the credit chain for 30 years. It needed to find a way of using its huge customer base in American households to continue to originate mortgages, but without expecting to hold onto the loans long after they had been successfully set up.

Suppose a bank was borrowing at 1.5% over the risk-free rate (the rate at which the government borrows for 25 years). Then a rational bond investor could buy a bond secured directly on the mortgages for the same rate (1.5% over governments) and enjoy the same return as the bank, including the margin for equity risk. So it is likely to be profitable for the bank to lend to the house-holder not at the bank's borrowing rate plus 1.5%, but at its own borrowing rate – 1.5% over the government borrowing rate – and then put a sizeable batch of mortgage loans so generated into a separate company and sell them directly to investors, who will take them on board as readily as the bank's own paper. The securities set up in this way are known as mortgage-backed securities (MBS) or more generally asset-backed securities (as, later, the loans put into them could be other items such as auto loans, credit card receivables and so on). The separate company is known as a special purpose vehicle (SPV – famous initials from asset-backed structures in the Enron case) or (more typically for recent mortgages) a structured investment vehicle (SIV).

The value of the 1.5% difference in borrowing cost from cutting out the bank's own balance sheet is large. For a loan of $100,000 over 30 years, with interest rates at 6%, a 1.5% interest differential has a present value of $16,500, one-sixth of the mortgage principal. A competitor bank could offer better terms to householders using this technique than a bank using its own balance sheet, and could still gain a portion of this value by selling the batch of loans to the SIV at a profit. Ultimately, competition forces down the cost of mortgages to householders to use up most of the present value from taking the bank out of the middle; but a portion remains to enable the loans to be packaged and sold in batches for a sum greater than their face value. This permits the bank to take origination fees, servicing fees (to gather the monthly payments, and so on) while releasing its capital and loan capacity for a new round of mortgages and fees.

This is level one, the mortgage-backed vehicle, such as an SIV. In recent years, with (until 2006) short-term interest rates well below longer-term (such as 25-year) rates, the search for more affordable mortgages to extend the range and depth of the market has brought into prominence mortgage loans with rates that vary over time. (This is the normal structure in Britain and Spain.) The loan still has a long life, but the interest rate – and therefore the householder's monthly payment – is reset when short-term rates change. This structure (when packaged in an SIV) makes possible periodic funding in the money markets, typically as commercial paper. Money-market investors (for example, People's Bank of China or its agent banks) might buy commercial paper with a short maturity, such as three months, secured on an SIV. If rates go up, the rates on the mortgages should rise to match the increased cost of funding, and vice versa.

How does SIV-backed commercial paper get repaid? By a new issue, of course. But what if Johnny Money-Market decides he does not want that commercial paper any more? To guard against that risk, the SIV has a 'back-stop' loan facility from the originating bank (or anyone else of suitable quality that wants to provide it). Meanwhile, as long as the SIV is out there in the market, funding itself with commercial paper, the mortgages are off the originator's balance sheet, and the usual fees have been taken early on to reflect the mortgage interest rate being somewhat above the rate demanded by the commercial paper investors.

Level two is asset-backed securities themselves secured on the level-one SIVs, or other MBSs. MBSs set up with this approach to funding do not need to be funded in the bond or money markets as they are funded by the proceeds of second-level asset-backed securities, known as 'collateralised debt obligations' (CDOs). The added value here arises from (for example) the investor appetite for high-grade, ideally AAA, securities, and the dearth of triple-A companies. If a batch of mortgages in an SIV can be expected on average to incur losses of 1% (the original premise above), it is a fair bet that a security having access to the first 95% of the cash flows is ultra-safe; 'as safe as houses' scarcely does it justice – this is safer than houses. If the normal recovery rate on the mortgages is 99% (face value of 100% less the 1% typical loss rate), what are the chances of failing to recover even 95%? Very small. A security that has first call on 95% of the cash flows is quite likely to be rated triple-A.

Suppose that a high, AAA rating lowers the interest rate at which a bond can be issued by 0.5%. We have already seen that a saving of 1.5% has a present value of 16½% of the loan principal: one-third of that is worth more than 5½%. Add that profit to the 95% of face value involved and the deal has already yielded more than 100% of face value. The remaining 5% of the principal of the SIV – including practically all the risk – can be sold off at a discount and the whole deal is profitable. The SIV has been split into at least two second-level CDOs: the 'senior', AAA portion, and the junior rump. That rump was generally – to maximise the value of the deal – split into at least two pieces: the better part of it, limited to the amount of the principal (after the 'AAA' first 95% in the example) that could be rated single-A or at worst BBB (at which levels it still counted as 'investment-grade') was known as the 'mezzanine' tranche; the rest was known as the 'equity' tranche, and, being virtually certain to be hit by proportionately large losses, has been nicknamed 'toxic waste'.

CDOs that were issued were a function of the ratings they were deemed to merit, that is, by rating agency models of the likely default rate. A triple-A CDO could perfectly well contain the better portion of the risk from some good-quality mortgages, some low-quality mortgages, some asset-backed securities based on consumer credit – anything really, so long as it could be rated. The portion of the SIV or other asset-backed paper that could be declared AAA (or the mezzanine, single-A/BBB level) would depend on the expected default rate in the basic credit: mortgage, auto loan, or whatever. So the 95% used in the example above relates to good-quality mortgages. For lesser-quality credits, the portion that rating agencies could declare AAA or AA would be less. The appetite for high-rated paper, and the absence of enough high-rated companies, created demand for the senior, AAA or AA tranches of CDO. Also many pension funds and other institutional investors are constrained in buying bonds to those that are (only or mostly) at least investment-grade (BBB or above). This constraint helped demand for the mezzanine tranches, making the CDO system even more original and effective.

Clearly, rating agency competence and probity are central to the viability of the CDO market. No evidence on the issue of probity has yet emerged to cause the kind of trouble to the rating agencies that beset the Arthur Anderson worldwide auditing partnership after Enron imploded. However, it is likely that there will be numerous lawsuits against them by aggrieved buyers of CDOs who have suffered losses. The above examples show that the quantity of banking fees that can be taken out at the front end of the deal is extremely sensitive to the difference between the rate on the underlying mortgages and the rate end-investors will accept owing to favourable ratings. Investment bankers are not shrinking violets in pursuit of their interests. The rating agencies would be under intense pressure to give favourable ratings to securities whose issuers were paying their fees.

When it comes to competence, the rating agencies are most easily criticised. Ratings such as triple-A were awarded through the use of models, generally the same ones the investment banks promoting the schemes had originated. The absence of previous experience of such structures should have enforced caution. For example, the mortgage brokers adopted the habit of offering 'piggy-back' second mortgages to householders. These were basically a means of enabling the householder to do without equity: if the senior mortgage being offered was 80% of the house's value, the piggy-back, second loan would cover the remaining 20%. Yet rating agencies appear to have attached the same expected default rate to these piggy-back mortgages as to earlier-era primary mortgages. Aside from its obvious implausibility, this raises at least two questions on competence and probity:

- Should the agencies have been offering such economically significant ratings at all, given the speculative nature of the default models in utterly new and extravagant conditions?
- Were the agencies too close in interest to the sponsoring investment banks (versus the dispersed universe of investors) to show the required disinterest in formulating a rating?

The last twist to the saga was 'teaser' rates on mortgages (see page 33). (The CDO system was elaborated into CDO^2 – CDOs constructed using other CDOs as the asset-backed vehicles, rather than SIVs or whatever. Onto all of this were piled 'credit default swaps' or CDSs – essentially, insurance contracts against defaults of anything at all, including often CDOs. These will be of great interest to Wall Street historians and probably anthropologists, but represent more detail than is needed here.) These teaser mortgages, to a large extent taken out by poor and often ignorant borrowers, could be passed off by the mortgage broker with the thought: 'Never mind the impact of the high payment in two years' time: house prices will have gone up and you can always refinance then with a new teaser mortgage.'

Unless, of course, the mortgage market has blown up in the interim. Note the (probably sincere) assumption that house prices would go up for ever – by at least the 4–5% a year needed to keep the loan principal outstanding at or behind the value of the house that is its collateral. But house prices – as seen above (page 28) – had stopped rising and were edging downward from September–October 2005. After the massive contradictions of the continued growth of household mortgage debt on the assumption of ever-rising house prices had started to be appreciated even by the artists of denial most involved in it (in February 2007), conditions on new mortgages tightened up dramatically. (Or were introduced, in the case of the Ninja – 'no income, no job or assets' – mortgages that had also been put in place, also conveniently without documentation either.) The refinancing game was up – especially for the low-quality, sub-prime borrowers needing (as it turned out) over 100% of their home's value by way of refinancing loan.

The two-year teaser period in mortgages is a pipeline of impending defaults. The peak of unsound mortgage issuance was in 2006, when the end of house-price increases should have, but did not, lead to rapidly decelerating mortgage activity. Instead the teaser structure, which had until 2005 been used as a desirable inducement to householders to borrow, became a necessity for those involved in the mortgage business, even though they must surely have known that many of their borrowers' ability to repay was minimal or non-existent. Defaults on US mortgages in 2006 were over 800,000. In 2007, the total could be around 1.5 million, with the same again in 2008.

In the face of this disaster, the SIV and CDO markets have gone through the usual stages of denial, anger and despair. The SIVs directly financed by the commercial paper market have found their funding sources gone, and have fallen back on facilities from the sponsoring banks – whose proud claim to have got the loans off their balance sheets has proved vain. The CDO market is floundering in near-total ignorance of how to value CDOs. The precise composition of the assets backing the vehicles whose varying-quality tranches are in the CDOs is hard to determine. At the least it requires substantial research: not at all the same thing as relying on a rating agency ranking. Double-A paper from as late as July 2007 has changed hands for well under 50% of face value – a complete contradiction of the meaning of double-A.

Should anyone care? Clearly those who believed the salesmen's chatter and are now duly being separated from their money will. More importantly, swaths of mortgages, MBSs and CDOs have come back onto banks' balance sheets and are both tying up capital and freezing their ability to make loans. It is not just the influx of such assets that is causing a seize-up of the whole global credit system, but the simple fact that nobody knows what they are worth. This arises from another hugely important issue in what has happened – the loss of 'transparency'.

Another bomb yet to drop is hedge funds' holdings of CDOs and other instruments. These are estimated to be about one-third of the amounts held in the United States, larger than the holdings of banks, unlike in Europe and Asia where the investors lured in were mostly banks. (Good data on the distribution are not available, and other estimates of the hedge fund portion are higher. But the position is further complicated by many hedge fund holders allegedly having options to put their CDOs or SIVs back to the originating commercial banks.) While banks have gone a long way down the road of 'owning up' to the write-offs they are going to have to make – not least because they are supervised and have to produce quarterly or semi-annual accounts for shareholders – the silence of the hedge funds has been deafening. Investors in hedge funds will let the devil take the hindmost: they can cash out before the hedge funds have disclosed their losses on CDOs and suchlike and may escape their share of them, leaving their share of the losses to those left holding the baby. To the opacity of the multiple layers of instruments making up this mortgage derivative debacle is added the opacity of the affairs of one the largest group of investors in them, the hedge funds.

The theory of disclosure is that it benefits investors of all stripes. Disclosure has for the most part been introduced to protect investors, for example to prevent insiders taking advantage of privileged information. But disclosure should raise the value of investments for insiders too. It reduces uncertainty, and so lessens the risk premium in the required rate of return from an investment. For a given cash flow in that investment, a lower risk premium – and therefore a lower rate of return – will mean a higher price. (For example, a cash flow of $5 is worth $100 if the required rate of return is 5%, but it is worth $125 if the required return is only 4%, $5 being 4% of $125.) That higher price will benefit all investors, insiders and outsiders.

In a culture of non-disclosure, however, insiders who make

a voluntary 'first move' towards extra disclosure may be losers, especially in investment funds where some positions are bound to go wrong and the managers need to preserve a strong reputation. This is one reason why public authorities are so often involved in setting disclosure requirements, or at least supervising adequate self-regulation by an industry. But opacity, though bad for prices in the long run, can help generate upward price pressure in irrational bull markets. Thus in the late-1990s bubble, numerous firms were set up with only the vaguest disclosure of what they were actually going to do to generate revenue and profit; but the very absence of information attracted investors hoping to find the pot of gold at the end of the rainbow. Full disclosure of how little prospect there was of results would have put the mad bulls off – the absence of any track record became an advantage in attracting funds. Similarly with hedge funds, managers with good track records offer minimal information: investors can 'take it or leave it'.

The US mortgage debacle is likely to cause major losses in hedge funds that are in many cases owned (directly or ultimately) by such institutions as state-employee pension funds. It is hard to believe that an industry that has moved so far into the mainstream where 'widows and orphans' are affected will escape regulation. Nor should it, in the matter of disclosure. How far the regulation will go in terms of other burdens is another matter. The record is not encouraging. The Sarbanes-Oxley rules in the United States, responding to the Enron scandal, have been badly aimed, excessive and counter-productive, as before them was the Glass-Steagall Act of the 1930s, responding to the 1929 crash. But the shift towards greater disclosure and transparency is essential. If that means the sheer complication of asset-backed mortgage structures and their derivatives puts people off – or causes them to trade badly and thus chokes off new issuance – then so much the better. People should not be buying investments they do not understand.

Staggering US mortgage losses

How big is the US sub-prime mortgage problem? Websites tracking foreclosures indicate that the US-wide total of loans foreclosing was running at 2½ million in 2007, up by 70% from around 1½ million in 2006. The level of defaults is actually only a little over 60% of the foreclosures because many defaulters have two (or more) mortgages on their houses: for example, the recent practice of the first mortgage to cover 80% of the house's value, and the need for householder's equity being avoided by taking out a piggy-back loan for the remaining 20%. Another practice is for householders with spare equity in their houses to take out a second-mortgage facility to finance other expenses. The 60% ratio means that defaults rose from over 800,000 in 2006 to around 1½ million in 2007.

In 2008, the rate of teaser mortgage resets (to normal repayment) reaches its peak in the second quarter and then tails off. So a further 1½ million defaults can reasonably be expected. With more to come in early 2009, the spring-2009 total over three and a bit years should be around 4 million. At roughly $200,000 per defaulting household, the total of mortgages going under could be $800 billion.

The savings and loans debacle in 1990–93 showed recoveries averaging 80% on defaulting mortgages. But loans in those days were made at around 80% of the value of the house, so the recoveries were some 64% of the value of the house (80% of 80%). Now the loans going bad are ones made typically at 100% of the value of the house. This suggests recoveries could be less than two-thirds of the principal owed this time round, with losses of over one-third of the mortgages in default. This would amount to $250 billion–300 billion. A similar estimate was reached by analysts at the Organisation for Economic Co-operation and Development (OECD, the industrial countries' Paris-based economic research institute) in November 2007, using default rates applied to the total of mortgage resets in 2007 and 2008.

The process of recovery could enlarge this forecast total of losses, as could the way they have been reprocessed into SIVs, CDOs and the like. The packaging of mortgages into asset-backed securities takes away the originating bank's traditional role of lender and substitutes the role of collecting agent for the holder (the SIV, CDO or whatever). In the traditional system, once a debtor stopped paying the monthly amount under the mortgage, the bank would quickly act to sort things out: either with a rescheduling or restructuring of the person's debts, or with a repossession and foreclosure sale. But as agent for some entity holding the mortgage against a chain of asset-backed securities the bank feels little urgency, as it has less to lose from default. Its response is likely to be much slower. And the flexibility that a bank has in relation to mortgages held on its own books may be absent when it is acting under legal asset-backed loan documentation as agent for the SIV, CDO (or whatever). Work-outs that recover all or much of the loan's value may not be permissible – or may be prevented by the delays in the processing of the default.

The second aspect of the new set-up that may increase losses is that the creation and sale to investors of the SIVs, CDOs, and so forth made a profit for the commercial and investment banks involved, as described above. This was taken in the form of large fees. The amounts owed to investors by SIVs and CDOs exceed the principal value of the underlying mortgages. Those amounts will be additional losses in the string of forthcoming defaults. For these reasons the total of losses could easily be larger than the $250 billion–300 billion estimated above.

The financial sector has conducted a vain rearguard action against the implications of such losses. The value of CDOs and the like has slumped. But the $250 billion–300 billion number, originally estimated by myself and my colleague Diana Choyleva at Lombard Street Research in the summer of 2007, is now widely accepted. Although its incidence is dispersed (in Europe, hedge funds, investment banks, and so on), it must be compared with US commercial bank capital of $1 trillion, and 2006 pre-tax profits of $190 billion. Even spread over two or three years, the impact is likely to be huge – though not crippling – and the future flow of profits will be also be cut by the likely lower levels of business and fees. The interbank market has come close to seizing up as investors shied away from exposure to even the most reputable banks – non-disclosure taking its toll. Bank shares are heavily down, and waves of financial crisis flow through the markets with each new unpleasant revelation. *Quis custodiet ipsos custodies –* or, who guards the guardians? For many countries, the backstop, or guardian, is the central bank.

3

Central banks fumble

The Goldilocks economy (see pages 28–9), with globalisation providing downward pressure on inflation, was rendered even more easily manageable for central banks by the provision of liquidity from savings-glut countries. Earlier, during the 1990s, inflation was curbed independently of central banks by consistently high real bond yields, which helped prevent excessive credit growth. Bond yields remained much higher than usual relative to inflation partly because of the losses bond investors suffered during 1970–81's 'Great Inflation' – 'never again' was the reaction. Also inflation coming in consistently below expectations itself made real interest rates higher in the outcome than had perhaps been intended. In 2007 central banks saw the end of the easy years. Their response to new challenges is far from adequate.

In August 2007, the European Central Bank (ECB) and the Fed got off to a good start. First off the blocks was the ECB, when huge exposures to CDOs and other instruments emerged (most conspicuously) at German banks. After serious trouble in June–July, Bear Stearns closed down two hedge funds that were invested in sub-prime mortgage paper, and the money-market access for SIVs to commercial paper funding started to shrink. The banks' access to interbank deposits in the money markets came under threat, and the interbank rates (London InterBank Offer Rate, Libor, in various currencies) mounted well above policy rates – the 'repo rate' (then 4%) in the case of the ECB. The suspicion with which banks were being treated by investors (and other banks) turned out to be justified. Some state-owned German banks had to be bailed out. The ECB had to make available emergency liquidity of no less than €95 billion to ensure smooth settlement of interbank borrowing requirements.

The difference between liquidity problems and bankruptcy is normally important, but it did not matter in this case. The ECB did its job of ensuring no general systemic damage arose from problems at particular banks. In general, any intervention to bail out the banks themselves, if they were insolvent, should have occurred only if the managements were replaced and the shareholders left with nothing. But in this case, the shareholder was the general public so the loss was for the taxpayers' account anyhow. The taxpayers in question were mostly German, suffering from the poor management of their public-sector banks. In other countries, particularly the United States and Britain, banks are privately owned, so the distinction between what is done to preserve liquid money markets and dealing with instances of bankruptcy is important.

The next test was passed equally well a week later, this time by the Fed. Seeing steadily rising interbank rates, it left its policy-target rate unchanged at 5¼%, but lowered the discount rate, at which it will supply funds to banks under liquidity pressure, from

6¼% to 5¾%. This last rate had just been exceeded by dollar Libor. But the Fed's move meant that banks could borrow unlimited funds at 5¾%, preventing Libor from mounting further – and were encouraged by the Fed to do so. Nevertheless, the Libor stayed close to 5¾%, whereas the Fed's target for interbank funds was 5¼%. So in mid-September it lowered both the target funds rate and the discount rate by ½%, with the effect that the discount rate came down to the old target funds rate of 5¼%, bringing Libor down with it and getting short-term interest rates back on target. So far, so good.

At this point, the pressure began to expose central-banking weaknesses. In Britain, the Bank of England (BoE) had been talking firmly in public about loss-making banks having to take their medicine. Unfortunately, it was not adequately aware of growing liquidity problems at a medium-sized mortgage lender, Northern Rock. Back in 1998, a year after the BoE had been given independence to control monetary policy, control of bank regulation and supervision was taken away from it. The Financial Services Authority (FSA), the agency in charge of bank supervision, failed to make Northern Rock's liquidity problems known to the BoE. These erupted into public view, causing a run on a bank for the first time in Britain since the 19th century. Emergency funding for Northern Rock became essential without any prior stipulation about removing the management and ensuring shareholders took the rap. The big talk about delinquent banks taking their medicine looked silly, and the British reputation for good economic policy was justifiably dented – the chief mistake (made by the prime minister, Gordon Brown, in his previous job as Chancellor of the Exchequer) being division of bank supervision from monetary policy.

Competitive devaluation and inflation

The Fed then moved in October from compensating for market disruption to easing policy. Financial markets had interpreted its September move as deliberate easing, and their assessment of the Fed's attitude was vindicated by the October cut of ¼% in the policy-target funds rate and the discount rate, to 5% and 4½%, respectively. This move did more harm than good. Economic growth in the middle quarters of 2007 was above the 3% 'speed limit' and inflation was and is at or above the 2% ceiling of the Fed's 1–2% 'comfort zone'. The apparent goals of the Fed's move were either or both of dollar devaluation and outdoor relief for bankers. The dollar proceeded to slide and oil prices to soar, making the inflation problem worse. The Fed's signal that Wall Street's problems may be worse than banks themselves had yet chosen to disclose led borrowing rates for the general public and for business (unlike the government) to rise: together with dearer oil this risked worsening economic growth, not conserving it, alongside worse inflation.

A key point is that the combination of events does not permit an optimal Fed policy. The most that can be achieved is offsetting different goals against one another. One factor is that excessive credit and monetary growth was encouraged by the Fed, which had held the target funds rate at 1% until as late as June 2004, and then only raised it to 5¼% over two years in ¼% increments at each of eight meetings a year plus one further, for a total of 17 small moves. The backwash from that is likely to require tougher policy. Rising oil prices and a falling dollar mean both higher inflation and lower real income growth at home – that is, stagflation, the curse of the oil crises of the 1970s. Experience shows that targeting low inflation deals with stagflation better than muddling around between inflation and growth objectives. In its current dilemma, lowering interest rates to revive borrowing hardly seems a good idea when at the root of the crisis lies excessive debt to start with. The Fed's dramatic easing in early 2008 is unlikely to help growth and employment, and is certain to increase inflation – at the expense of future growth: the long, ghastly 1970–82 experience taught us that once financial markets and the general public become convinced high inflation is here to stay, trend growth rates slow down and the structural, inflation-neutral unemployment rate rises, adding to the misery caused by the inflation itself.

The Fed's policy does not just threaten worse inflation for the United States while probably somewhat harming growth too. This reaction to Wall Street panic designed to head off domestic political pressures may do international damage too. The context is that the world badly needs China to accept much faster appreciation of the yuan. This may be (as argued here, see page 17) in China's domestic interest anyhow, but the chorus of advice from abroad is clearly self-serving. Why should China worry about foreign opinion when the Fed so clearly puts America's sectional interests ahead of its own broader economic policy goals (low inflation and growth)?

The context very much includes memories of the Asian Crisis. When Asian countries got into financial trouble ten years ago, the clear policy enforced by American policymakers was deflation without regard to the domestic consequences in Asia. China, unlike most of developing Pacific Asia, weathered that storm, but watched the consequences for the other regional economies with horror. The policy was extremely severe, and the only clear beneficiaries of it were the international banks that had lent to the stricken countries. All of a sudden, when the US financial system is in trouble, who appears to get the greatest benefit from US government policy? The international banks. Deflation that was thoughtlessly meted out to Asian countries in trouble became unthinkable for America – a point that may have been taken in Beijing, diminishing the chance that foreign pressure on its policy will have any effect. More dangerously, competitive devaluation of the dollar may reinforce the more mercantilist Chinese policymakers who believe in a low exchange rate as an article of faith: it is evidence that the Fed, in its heart of hearts, agrees with them.

A broader point arises from the world's need for Chinese policy that takes some measure of responsibility for the international system. Competitive devaluation was one of the policy blunders that contributed to the Great Depression in the 1930s. At that time true economic power had crossed the Atlantic to America, but without the Americans being aware that they had unwittingly become custodians of the world's good economic order. Now economic power has passed to a remarkable degree and with startling suddenness across the Pacific to China – in a way it never did in the days of apparent Japanese ascendancy in the 1980s. This is hardly the time to be discouraging the outward-looking Chinese. Their more chauvinist counterparts in Beijing's internal debates should not be handed easy nationalistic arguments. It is important to understand that the forthcoming series of what will probably end up being thought of as central bank stumbles (preferably not blunders) will be no more entirely their fault than the good reputation they gained in 1996–2006 was truly to their credit. Without China buying into the global system and accepting its share of responsibility for it, failure is highly likely.

4

US economic slowdown: house prices sap confidence

Although the US economy was surprisingly resilient in the second and third quarters of 2007, the Fed was reasonable in anticipating a slowdown. The growth of incomes in the later stages of the boom became highly dependent on unconventional sources of pay, rather than wages and salaries in monthly pay packets. Half the growth in labour income per hour consisted of gains in such exotic elements as real estate commissions (now in full retreat), annual bonuses and stock-option profits. Bonuses are now threatened, at least in their growth. Stock options now coming up for exercise are tending to have higher 'strike' prices than previously: the profit per option could be less. Without these sources of growth, income could rise little more than the rate of inflation.

Perhaps more seriously, the effect on wealth could be extremely negative. By end-2007, the broadest and best measure of house-price inflation was already down 7–8%. Realised prices in existing home transactions held up until early summer. This is traditional in housing downswings – they are slow burners and take years.

At the start of such phases, householders 'know' that their house is worth the highest number they have ever heard attributed to it. But transaction prices were sustained at the expense of a shrinking volume of deals. The overhang of unsold homes is about ten months' worth of sales. Have you ever sold a home and found it took ten months? The wear and tear on the nerves is intense.

The 2007 credit crisis not only took the wind out of the stockmarket's sails and made conditions on new mortgage advances even more arduous than they had become from February 2007, when awareness of the sub-prime issue first surfaced – it also told the American public that the game truly was changed. Even for existing home transaction prices the rot set in. Prices dropped 5% in the early autumn. The combination of a shaky stockmarket, tough mortgage loan conditions and falling house prices can only mean a sharp drop in both capacity and appetite for household debt, despite the initial pre-Christmas reaction of 'eat, drink, and be merry – for tomorrow we die'. The prospect of major housing repossessions by mortgage lenders, and resulting sales and depression of prices in many neighbourhoods, could reinforce this until well into 2009 at least. Consumer spending could therefore fall behind real income growth. But as the latter is likely to be minimal, a consumer recession is the logical result. An important point of short-term timing is that bonus payments and stock-option exercise are heavily concentrated in December and January, so that these powerful income and consumer-confidence factors are frequently ignored until they are palpable in people's pockets in the new year.

An important result of the sub-prime debacle is serious

tightening of credit and money. Fed policy has compensated for the upward drift of money-market rates (at the expense of aggravating an already serious inflation, soon to be stagflation, problem), but other effects remain. Most obviously, new mortgages are much more reluctantly given, with tougher conditions. The loan market for leveraged buy-outs (LBOs) was closed down by the banks' discovery of the sub-prime 'black hole' in their books. Banks had to stop all new lending until they could clarify their exposures. Yet private equity LBOs were the chief source of buying in the stockmarket until summer 2007. Their revival is almost bound to be on a smaller scale than before. The spread of interest rates between ten-year Treasuries and junk bonds has more than doubled as a result of the credit crunch. While bank capital is already being bolstered by inflows from China and the Middle Eastern oil states, its erosion is also holding back new loan growth. These shifts are bound to inhibit stock prices, contributing to weak consumer confidence, quite apart from directly reducing the flow of labour income in financial and related industries.

US housing construction should continue to drop like a stone well into 2008. As its decline levels out during the year it could be replaced by falling business spending as a depressant to private demand. But government spending – in an election year – should provide a cushion for total demand, and some of the pain of private demand cuts could be spread abroad by reduced imports: much higher oil prices and a higher-value euro point this way too. The big help to the United States from exports could fade, however, as European growth is likely to slow (see Chapter 4) followed by China later in 2008. The United States may avoid a recession in the sense of GDP being down from the same quarter in 2007. But for householders it could be a worse experience than a conventional recession: it is their spending that is expected to bear the brunt, as their balance sheets buckle under the combination of excessive debt and falling asset values.

It never rains, but it pours. Just as the real income of Americans is being reduced by higher external prices, as the dollar declines and prices of oil and food soar, underlying US growth is being slowed by lower productivity growth. It is these decidedly reduced prospects for Americans' standard of living that create a political threat. The primary crucial policy decisions on which a good recovery from the current world downswing depends are likely to be Chinese. But continued US openness to imports, and lessened resistance to foreign ownership of so-called sensitive industries, will also be important. The self-destructive nature of import restrictions is so obvious that it must be hoped they will be minimal: raising the cost of imports will increase inflation, lowering the US standard of living, and forcing the Fed to adopt a more restrictive monetary policy. Restricting Chinese purchases of US firms has less obvious costs – and America is almost as socialist as France in this area. Reductions in the standard of living usually make people angry – and they seldom blame themselves. In a US election year the scope for demagoguery is obvious. If policy in any respect drifts further towards economic nationalism, the downswing will be prolonged and medium-term recovery prospects will be weakened.

5

Decoupled wishful thinking

Voltaire's Dr Pangloss ('All's for the best in the best of all possible worlds') was clearly a good, fertile breeder, as the financial world is full of his descendants, together with those of Dickens's Mr Micawber ('Something will turn up'). In a desperate attempt to avoid the downside of globalisation – the world being connected up – its most conspicuous beneficiaries, financiers, are suggesting that the boom can go on – in developing Asia, in Europe, anywhere – because the global economy has become 'decoupled'. This is code for the hope that a US-based financial crisis and economic hard landing will not spread elsewhere.

Global linkage takes three forms: migration, trade in goods and services, and capital flows. Of these, the first reacts slowly, and is unlikely to be much affected by cyclical ups and downs, as opposed to long-term differences in trend between economies – with different levels of income being probably even more important than growth trends. Trade in goods and services is the traditional means by which US cycles have affected the rest of the world. However, the most thoroughly integrated global market is not for goods and services but for capital, the international flows of which have become huge and almost instantaneous as a result of globalisation and new technology.

If we take decoupling in its wishful-thinking meaning of not being dragged down by the US housing slump and its consequences, Europe and Asia are in different situations. Europe is largely decoupled from the United States on the trade front but closely integrated with it in capital flows: while weaker exports to the United States arising from its slowdown are unlikely to have much impact on the European economy, an indirect effect of that slowdown, the sharp rise in the euro (and the pound), is indeed likely to pass weakness across the Atlantic. Given a broad-based 'western' slowdown, Asian exporters (Japan, China and the Tigers) are highly likely to be affected, though in the Chinese case largely to remove gross overheating rather than cause a slump. But their stockmarkets have the ability to go their own way for other reasons, as explained below.

Europe: slowing as its currencies rise

The issue of coupling and decoupling takes very different forms in Europe and developing Asia. In western Europe as a whole, exports 'out of area' (that is, not to other countries in western Europe) are about 12–13% of GDP, but half of these are to the former Comecon countries: central-eastern Europe and the former Soviet Union. The export exposure of western Europe to the Americas, Asia and the rest of the world is only some 6% of GDP: about half, 3%, to the United States, the remainder to the rest. Variations in the growth of an item that is 3% of GDP are minimally significant in themselves. Europe's economy appears largely decoupled from the United States.

Capital market integration between Europe and the United States, however, is greater than ever. Indeed, the scale of European exposure to US sub-prime mortgage derivatives was almost comic. US problems are likely to affect Europe via the price mechanism, not the volume effect of lesser American imports – that is, via the rising euro–dollar exchange rate and also the dollar exchange rates for the pound, Swiss franc and Scandinavian currencies which have risen more or less in tandem with the euro. While Germany and the surrounding countries that are a major part of the Eurasian savings glut – Benelux, the Nordic group and Switzerland/Austria – may prove able to handle rising foreign-exchange rates, the same may not be true of France, Italy and Spain, where business is a good deal less competitive. Italy and Spain in particular need devaluation of their real exchange rates (that is, after adjustment for relative inflation) and are getting the opposite. In Britain, Spain and Ireland, variations on the US overblown housing and household debt crisis are also developing, reinforcing the effects of their overvalued currencies.

The growth rate trend in Europe is hardly impressive to start with. It has improved since 2005 as Germany has put behind it the massive adjustments needed after reunification and the resultant structurally excessive labour and other costs. But for the euro-zone countries, the growth trend probably averages only about 2%, maybe a touch more, with 2½% in Britain, Denmark and Sweden, hold-outs against the euro. The west European economy has been growing faster than its trend 'speed limit' since 2005, and this has already led the central banks to raise interest rates several times. The credit crunch, which affected the euro and sterling Libor interbank interest rates as much (or more) than the dollar Libor, has added further monetary restrictiveness – and rising exchange rates are adding a third dollop. During 2008 European growth is likely to fall below trend, significantly so in Britain (see page 70) and more modestly in the euro zone.

Pacific Asia: a case of recoupling

In developing Asia, the story is the other way round: the economies depend on the United States more than does Europe, but the capital markets should be able to continue to thrive in anything but the short term. One-fifth of China's exports are to the United States and slightly more to Europe. With the United States close to recession and Europe growing below trend, China's export growth has to slow (at least). Its gains in export market share may also become less readily tolerated by Americans and Europeans in a tougher economic climate. This takes us to the global policy discussion (page 95), but it is safe to conclude that (even without a major upward realignment of the yuan) China's export growth will be much slower in future than it has been since 2003.

Other Pacific Asian Tigers are as badly placed. Some, such as Malaysia, are themselves heavily dependent on the United States. Others are less exposed, but will lose out from any slowing of exports from China, which are often made up of parts made elsewhere, notably Japan, South Korea and Taiwan. These countries are taking more action than in the past to stimulate their domestic economies, in sharp contrast to Japan (see pages 72–4), but they remain savings-glut countries in surplus on a scale that is changing only slowly. A savings glut can be restated as a structural tendency to under-spend income. If the export trade eases off, their economies will continue to enjoy their current strong growth only if policy is shifted further towards domestic stimulation.

India is quite different. It is less export dependent than China and the Tigers, and its exports are largely services (high-tech, outsourcing, and so on). It also has no shortage of domestic demand and no structural surplus. Its economy is overheated and is rightly being reined in (though not enough) by tighter monetary policy. But this is domestic rebalancing, and has nothing to do with tougher conditions in the United States or elsewhere. India is the only Asian economy that is relatively decoupled in the trading sense.

In capital markets it is a matter of recoupling rather than decoupling. The decoupling took place ten years ago, in the Asian crisis. Non-Japan Asian stockmarkets have not done well from their post-emergence peak in mid-1994 (see Figure 12). With July 1994 as 100, the Morgan Stanley–Capital International index for non-Japan Asia (in US dollar terms) fell to about 30 in the Asian crisis, rose substantially (but well short of 100) by the bubble-peak in 2000, and was then back down to 30 again in 2002–03 at the trough. Since then this index has risen five times to 150. Five times in 4–5 years or so is great performance. But up 50%

Figure 12 **MSCI emerging Asia US$ index**

Source: Morgan Stanley – Capital International

(nominal) in 13 years is dismal, worse than US Treasury bills with far more risk. Until the end of 2006, the index remained below its July 1994 level – nil return over 12 and half years.

It may be a bit early to be sure these markets have truly recoupled, rather than merely recovered a portion of the ground lost in the decoupling, which occurred a long time ago, in 1994–99, and in the wrong direction. But the signs are fair, and the faster growth rates of the region mean that America's sub-prime afflictions may be shrugged off (with a little help from Asian investors, who have been more cautious than European investors in buying CDOs and so on). What the poor performance of the past 13 years makes clear – in the context of economies enjoying historically superb growth – is that current stock price levels are no bubble. Boom maybe – with a bear market to come, maybe – but only a major war is likely to prevent them achieving reasonable medium-term growth.

Shifting from the Tigers in general, and India, to China, Shanghai 'A' stocks are at a substantial premium to the same stocks as quoted in Hong Kong, outside the exchange-control wall; and they are on price/earnings (p/e) ratios of 40–50. The p/e is only that low because of earnings being swollen by companies' 'Zaitech'-style crossholdings of one another's shares that yield profits in a price upswing. Both this and the premium to the global-market quote in Hong Kong suggest overvaluation. Here too the market has been called a bubble – with more justification, as Chinese demand for stocks is largely bottled up in the domestic market, unable to flow abroad.

But casual use of the word 'bubble' is lazy and unconvincing. Suppose the 'true' p/e ratio is not 40–50, but a massive 100 (that is, suppose half the apparent earnings are false). Then the earnings yield is 1%. Adding in China's GDP growth trend of 9.7% implies that the all-in potential yield of Chinese stocks would be in double figures, once any actual dividend yield (or other distributable free cash flow, for example by stock buy-back in the market) is added to growth to generate all-in, total real yield. That implies a decent 3–4% premium to the long-run S&P (that is, US) real stockmarket return of 6½–7%. Obviously, investing in Chinese stocks involves substantial risks – not just economic, or even those related to 'governance' issues, but also because the value of the majority-state-owned stocks that are a large part of the Shanghai 'A' index is frequently and arbitrarily changed by government actions. But the general point remains: any free cash flow from stocks in an economy growing at a trend rate of nearly 10% is a plus. And a real potential yield in the 10% region looks even better when the domestic investor's alternative is minus 3% from bank deposits, as in China.

Britain, Spain, Ireland and Japan in trouble

If we treat Spain as a virtual island, there is a trio – a quartet if Ireland is included – of peripheral islands around major continental blocs with their own special problems that could worsen the global effects of the credit crunch. In the European cases, housing and real estate in general is the chief issue, as these economies followed the US approach of 'using up' the Eurasian savings glut with a credit-based housing boom. Japan continues its tradition of at least the past 20 years of being in a unique economic situation.

Looking at the US housing disaster zone, we can distinguish different elements, which are present in varying degrees in Britain and Spain (see Table 2).

Balancing these various factors, and setting them against the prospective world environment, Britain could go through the wringer in 2008, with a greater chance of recession than America. As well as the most excessive house prices and household debt among major economies, Britain has the highest interest rates and little real household income growth owing to inflation. It has been the most overheated during 2007, apart from perhaps China, and

Table 2 **Housing problems: the United States, Britain and Spain compared**

US	Britain	Spain
Excess household debt: 130% of disposable income	170% of disposable income, and subject to higher interest rates	130% of disposable income (same as the US and twice the end-1999 level)
Excessive housing construction: grew at a real 6% a year from the 2000 cyclical peak to the recent peak	Grew at only 3%	Grew at 6% (same as the US), and with housing at a higher share of GDP
Massive potential borrower defaults	Could be seriously affected	Major defaults unlikely
A house-price boom that could go bust	Price gains have been higher than in the US, and prices also higher	House prices are still 'affordable'
An undervalued dollar and good productivity growth to mitigate a downswing in the construction sector	Sterling heavily overvalued, but business productivity doing better than the dismal general performance of continental Europe	Serious cost and price overvaluation has compounded negligible productivity growth for the past ten years

is most exposed to the reversal of 'Goldilocks' economic conditions, having been their most conspicuous beneficiary, indeed the epicentre of globalisation, since the mid-1990s. But a major downswing of sterling is likely, making subsequent recovery probable, subject to the world economy in general.

Spain has a much more serious problem. What it needs is devaluation and tight monetary policy. What seem like quite high interest rates in 'core' Europe have seemed low in Spain, where growth and inflation are higher, and housing remains affordable by past standards. Meanwhile, the weak productivity growth of the past decade and strong labour cost gains argue for a lower exchange rate to facilitate recovery, as in Britain. But Spain has neither a currency of its own nor a monetary policy. It will have to accept the probably high-valued euro and lowish interest rates of the euro zone, the opposite of what it needs. Poor growth for several years can be expected.

Japan's prospective recession is quite different, largely reflecting a huge policy blunder. Japan should be the country best placed to sail through the current difficulties via domestic demand growth from a private sector largely without debt. Japan was the original savings-glut country from the mid-1990s, as its depressed population trends caused investment to fall and late-career saving to rise, followed by massive restructuring by businesses that found themselves by 1996 with a crippling debt load. By 2003–04, both household and business balance sheets were in excellent shape, and the start of retirement by bulge generations was cutting household savings down almost to American levels (that is, non-existent). Business 'saving' (depreciation plus retained profits) was 25% of GDP, twice the US level. Everything pointed to a spending surge and sustained recovery (see Figure 13).

Instead what happened was a massive claw-back of the

Figure 13 **Japanese private saving**
% of GDP

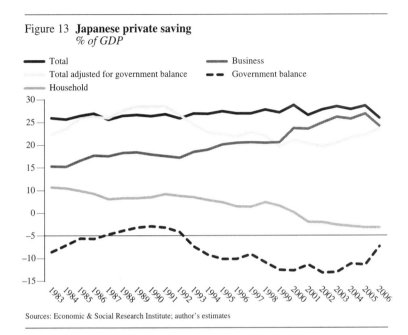

Sources: Economic & Social Research Institute; author's estimates

government deficit which outweighed the falling private surplus (that is, the true savings glut). This fiscal deflation was unnecessary, but the Japanese authorities thought they were offsetting it with easy money – continued close-to-nil interest rates. But there was a snag. The Japanese did not want to borrow: they already had their huge savings surplus. Japanese households have bank deposits three times as large (vis-à-vis GDP) as Americans do: what they wanted, to encourage spending, was high interest rates. So the low rates reinforced the deflationary impact of the fiscal claw-back.

What kept things on the move in 2006–07 was the falling yen. The cheap borrowing rates were irresistible to foreigners wanting cheap funding for low-yield or no-yield speculations like copper futures. Japanese investors wanting yield, but unable to get it in Japan, sent their money abroad for a better return. It was even a good capital return, as the borrowers could repay in depreciating yen, and Japanese investors got currency gains as well as yield. Both the world boom and the cheap yen ensured some export-led growth for Japan. But even that is liable to end, now that world growth is slowing down. And the yen is no longer so cheap as investors flee the dollar, repay their yen loans from increasingly worthless speculative positions and hold the yen as a proxy in case China unleashes the yuan.

'Commodity countries' unlikely to remain unscathed

Although investors around the world have been urged by investment bankers to have a 'flutter' in 'hard assets' – typically industrial commodities such as metals and oil – the proposal is directly contrary to economic theory and most past experience. It is much more likely that 2007 was the peak of a strong commodity upswing (see Figure 14) – from the depths achieved at the end of the Asian crisis in 1998–99 – and that most commodities, probably even including oil, will be going down in price over the next few years.

For renewable resources, usually based on crops, such as food or textiles ('soft' commodities), the argument is simple. Rising labour productivity over time cuts the number of worker-hours (the ultimate real-value measure) needed to produce a given unit

Figure 14 **US Commodity Research Board Indices**
Original indices deflated by US CPI, rebased to July, 1974 = 100

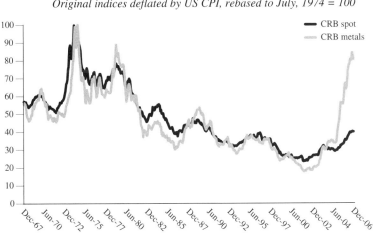

of the commodity. For metals and energy ('hard' commodities), finite resources and the increasing obscurity of fresh discoveries are a factor: miners 'top-slice' available reserves, going first for 'low-hanging fruit'. But gains in extraction technology and efficiency are still likely to reduce the real all-in cost of supplies over time. Prices may be driven up from time to time by strong demand, but supply can, or at least always has, ultimately rise to match: hardly surprisingly, since such prices offer super-profits vis-à-vis long-run total costs (including exploration).

Practical experience roughly bears out theory. The Commodity Research Board's total index since 1947 has increased by a factor of four, and its metals index by 12. The US CPI rose tenfold. Commodity prices experienced a lull in 1947, after the second world war and before the Korean war. Taking the 1974 peak of

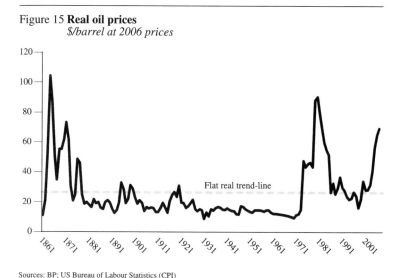

Figure 15 **Real oil prices**
$/barrel at 2006 prices

Flat real trend-line

Sources: BP; US Bureau of Labour Statistics (CPI)

these indices (at the end of the long post-war boom and just as the oil crises were starting to bite) as a base, progress since then has been distinctly less than that of the CPI, for metals as well as the total index. From the 1974 peak to the current peak, commodity prices are down in real terms, by a cumulative 19% for metals and 61% for the total index, both over 33 years.

The same cannot be said, purely on the basis of the past 60 years, of oil prices. Oil has been at the heart of the global political economy since the 1970s. At the moment, although its price boom is not as dramatic as in the two 1970s oil crises, rapid energy-intensive growth in developing Asia is raising prices. As a result, the real price trend since the 1950s is upward at a rate of about 2¼% a year. Examining oil prices over a longer span, going back to the 19th century on the basis of BP data, the trend-line of the real price is flat, neither rising nor falling (see Figure 15).

Forces in the recent world boom that have caused particularly large upswings in commodity prices include the following:

- Growth in the United States, Europe and Japan has been weak by boom-period standards, but growth has been unusually strong in developing Asia – not just China and the Tigers, but also India – and in some Latin American countries that have formerly been disappointing, especially Brazil.

- Developing Asian countries may have low labour costs, but they are wasteful of productive resources, generally controlling energy prices and often even subsidising them. The concentration of growth in such countries raises demand higher than would be normal for the rate of world growth we have experienced.

- China in particular was caught out with an inadequate power system in its 2003–04 boom and has hugely boosted power generation capacity since then. The telecoms industry may have substituted glass-fibre for copper, but the electricity industry still depends on copper.

- The demand side of the boom has been led by massive price increases in housing and property generally. This has led to an unusually strong construction boom: the construction industry is the biggest market for steel and many other metals and a major market for others, such as copper. The emergence of developing Asia has added to this global construction boom.

- A huge wave of portfolio investment has added another layer to these strong underlying demand-side forces, partly purely momentum

Figure 16 **Iron and steel prices**
1980 average = 100

Source: NE US scrap, Brazilian ore

based – 'let's buy what is going up' – but also increasingly driven by the theory that this is a new asset class. This is unsustainable, however, without a belief in severe and enduring limits on new supply.

These various points lead to the following conclusions: for oil, medium-term (five-year) price strength, but with a short-term cyclical downswing; for iron and steel, major short- and medium-term price weakness; for copper and base metals, a more severe price downswing than for iron and steel. Therefore the countries that have benefited heavily from strong commodity prices – including major economies such as Canada, Australia, South Africa and Brazil – are in for a harder time than recently.

6

The optimistic case: resolving the savings-glut imbalances

The Bill from the China Shop examined global imbalances from the late-2005 viewpoint and current woes were foreseen. Does this mean major imbalances are in principle unsustainable? No. The starting point for any empiricist must be that for 30 years up to the first world war – arguably the most prolonged global boom in history, and certainly the first – Britain, then the world's most advanced economy, and still one of its largest, ran current-account surpluses averaging over 5% of GDP. This earlier 'savings glut' was almost entirely beneficial, for both Britain and the rest of the world. What were the conditions that made this so?

Britain's reasons for running a savings glut before the first world war are of no great concern here. It may have reflected social, political or income-distributional defects of the country at that time, but Britain was a stable democracy in reasonable economic equilibrium. The ability of the rest of the world to absorb this flow of capital showed the scope that existed for development – in advanced countries such as the United States, in new countries such as Argentina, in resource countries within the British Empire such as South Africa and Australia, and even in India. The capital was in the form that the market indicated – equity and debt – although the bulk of the best investments were equity-related. As well as British willingness to export capital, there had to be proper treatment of foreign capital by the recipients. This was easy to ensure within the Empire, which covered a quarter of the world's area and population, but not elsewhere. Tales of US defaults on bonds can still be heard in the more obscure reaches of the City of London, and sovereign defaults did not have to await the takeover by the Bolsheviks of the Russian government in 1917.

In America, Britain and Spain, the danger is that 2008's hard landing will not lead to recovery. Housing downswings generally last five years, so even the US downswing, if it is dated from spring 2006 (when housing construction started to decline), has years to go. The mainspring of recovery has to be household spending. But household spending will no longer be able to depend on extra household debt, as in 2003–07, given the exhaustion of debt capacity and likely fears about the loss of wealth as house prices fall. So an alternative sector, government or business, will have to shift towards deficit to the extent that external deficits are maintained at or near current levels. Householders have too much debt, and their housing collateral is falling in value as house prices decline. The US economy may be stimulated by exports, after the devaluation of the dollar, but that will simply be preying on some other country's domestic demand – and probably not in savings-glut countries where it would be positive. Globally, the deficiency of demand that is the corollary of the savings glut could assert itself in the absence of household debt increases.

One way out will be government budget deficits. From a peak of 5% of GDP in 2003–04, the US deficit is now below 3%. In an election year like 2008, fiscal stimulation has quickly been promulgated. Spain has a substantial budget surplus, 2% of GDP, and no doubt will counter any economic downswing with either tax cuts or extra state spending or both. Britain's budget position is more parlous, as the deficit, already 3% of GDP, is pushing up close to the government's proclaimed 'golden rules' – which will simply have to be broken.

Fiscal stimulation will be useful, but by itself is unlikely to be enough. In a general world economic downturn, running up debt to finance growth of demand is likely to be replaced by debt deflation. Yet income growth itself will be slowed by the downturn. This means a double-whammy for demand, which has to shift from faster-than-income growth previously to slower-than-slower-income growth prospectively. Reinforcing this is the likelihood of business spending cuts as the downswing threatens profits and reveals spare capacity, while opportunities for profitable new investment are reduced. The only chance for recovery against this background will be if fiscal stimulation and lower interest rates can cut the burden on household budgets to ease debt service, leaving something for spending growth, and – and this is the crucial 'and' – major cuts in debt burdens are achieved by sale of equities. The danger is that, instead of this 'sound-money' approach to reducing debt burdens, Fed policy will instead shrink real debt via inflation, stagflation being a recipe for poor growth.

Turning to the savings glut, the chief point becomes: how fast will Eurasian savings-glut investors accept that the days of picking up purely debt obligations are over? In Asia, the shift towards a greater appetite for risk among Japanese investors has not been rapid, but it is there – despite 75–80% losses in 1990–2002 in both the stockmarket and house prices, for Japan 'the long night of the nineties'. The appetite of individual Chinese for stocks is beyond doubt. The issue therefore becomes a double-headed policy question. Will China's savings be unleashed onto world financial markets in some form other than passive money-market foreign-exchange reserve accumulation, and, if so, in what form and how fast? And will Chinese capital be welcomed by potential recipients, notably the United States, and given a 'fair break'?

The Eurasian savings glut started in 1998 as a result of the Asian crisis. (Before that it was a Japanese savings glut.) Its first destination was clear: the stockmarket. It helped blow up the bubble – especially in 'safe haven' America. As so often with overseas investment, the haven turned out not to be safe at all. As stockmarkets collapsed between mid-2000 and early 2003, the glut-savers headed for bonds and deposits. That was safe enough – and it needed to be, since much of the growth of the Eurasian surplus constituted Asian foreign-exchange reserves, destined for US Treasury bills and the like. That injection of liquidity (see page 138) underpinned the general lowering of interest rates, and later interest rate 'spreads' over Treasuries, that led to a huge upsurge of 'borrow-and-spend': on consumer goods and services, new homes, existing homes and real estate generally. The stockmarket recovered, but the chief destination of the funds was real estate. The current credit crunch and the US housing collapse that led to it have changed all that. Housing and real estate are overvalued and the supply of credit, fundamental to real estate strength, is severely inhibited.

What may be the new big thing?

The recent boom has been in emerging market equities and 'hard' assets, energy and commodities. Stocks generally are well sustained. Wall Street hit its all-time high as recently as September 2007, despite the collapse of housing, the resulting sub-prime-led credit crunch and the (by then already) expected knock-on into a general economic hard landing. The huge Asian savings flow that is financing America has now experienced losses in deposits and bonds; real estate is foundering and intermediaries face huge losses. But the financial market and (potential) economic weakness are pushing down interest rates and the dollar, helping Wall Street.

There are illusions here, of course. Domestic US profits are likely to be hit – it would be an odd economic downswing if they were not. And returns on US stocks are not so good when translated into real money: euros, for example. But the contrary force aiding stocks cannot be denied. The returns available to the huge flow of savings in Japan and China are low. Although the long-run real return on US equities has been 6½–7%, it is quite possible Asian investors would be happy with less than this. So the weight of money is there, to set against the likely earnings downswing. Hard assets and resource-country markets, helped by the blind push from the weight of money, are far less promising, as seen above (pages 74–8).

Who's got the money? China and Japan

A 'round-number' analysis of much of world savings is shown in Table 3.

Table 3 'Round-number' analysis of world savings, 2007

	GDP ($trn)	Savings rate (%)	Savings ($trn)
Western Europe[a]	17½	20	3½
US	13½	14	2
Japan	5	30	1½
China	3	50	1½

a EU–15, Switzerland and Norway.

Savings are national savings, not just household savings. They equal gross national income minus household and state-sector consumption. Looking at the first two lines in Table 3, it is consistent that western Europe's 20% savings ratio has yielded a small current-account surplus. Its peaking population and declining labour force mean that its investment needs are less than in the days of demographic expansion. The United States has a deficit of 5–6% of GDP, the external capital inflow compensating for low domestic savings. Japan and China are in structural surplus, approaching $200 billion and $400 billion respectively, that is, 4% and 13% of GDP. The rest of the world is in surplus of $100 billion–200 billion, more than fully accounted for by oil exporter surpluses.

What this crude analysis suggests is that the Chinese savers are potentially the largest untapped source of capital for world asset markets, followed by the Japanese. Also important at the moment are the oil producers, although their surpluses are likely, as in the past, to be cyclical – soon used up in spending, and reduced by lower oil prices in a world slowdown. The question is, therefore: what do the Chinese want?

For individuals in China the basic investment options are bank deposits, buying a flat or house, or buying Shanghai 'A' shares (which are available only to domestic investors, who are unable to buy shares outside China). As buying a flat or house is a one-off option and prices have become very high, fresh savings head for Shanghai 'A' or deposits, which typically pay rates of 4%, 3% below inflation. In other words, for Chinese individuals the baseline is a real return of –3%. This is not setting the bar high.

For Chinese businesses, which account for the largest part of the national savings total, the options are different. The negative real return on deposits is still important. But to some degree they can (or could) invest abroad – by subterfuge, if not overtly. Foreign direct investment is also a small but growing option. Using 'leads and lags' in export and import deliveries versus payments, they can lodge cash overseas. The problem is that they are confronted with a declining dollar – at 5% a year now, but potentially much more in an uncertain future, with the yuan beginning to rise even against the euro (against which it has so far gone down, given the euro's faster ascent). This means the leads and lags may be used more to buy yuan than to invest abroad – which takes businesses right back to the negative real Chinese interest rates.

Of course the primary Chinese overseas investor remains the government. Increases of reserves, by $550 billion in 2007, now amount to more than the current surplus, which is estimated to have been $361 billion–400 billion in 2007. This must mean net private capital flows are inward, not outward – confirming the point about firms speculating on yuan appreciation. So the bulk of capital exports remains People's Bank of China-sourced interest-bearing assets. But this is likely to change. The use this 'base-load' of global liquidity is put to by overseas intermediaries – hedge funds, private equity, intermediary borrowers in general – has also been shifting towards equities and 'hard assets'. In tandem, Japanese private investors and those other exporters of capital from Japan, the 'yen-carry' intermediaries, are slowly going the same way.

Why is the Chinese export of capital itself likely to change? There are a number of reasons. Europeans are soon likely to join their American counterparts in resisting China's naked mercantilism – huge gains in net exports with no attempt at justification in the form of capital exports, beyond passive reserve accumulation. Despite the slowdown in US imports in 2007, China's US-bound exports increased by 16%, albeit less than 2006's 25% gain. Further gains in a fast-slowing US economy, even at a lesser rate, could intensify dangerous protectionist pressures. But China's Europe-bound exports increased by 36% in 2007, well up from the previous year's 25%, and exceeded exports to the United States for the first time. This gave China an interest in the rise of the euro – in mercantilist mode, not as asset allocator. The rising euro, clearly favoured by the United States too, is the means by which the European economy could be seriously slowed in 2008, quite apart from the pain felt in industries displaced by aggressively priced Chinese imports. China has in effect joined the United States in a programme of competitive devaluation similar to that which worsened the 1930s Depression.

To give itself the best chance of deflecting US and European rage in 2008, China will need a major programme of unprovoked capital exports. The August 2007 initiative (since stalled) to allow Chinese individuals to invest abroad would be best broadened and extended rapidly. It has numerous advantages over the rational alternative already under way: national asset allocation within a sovereign investment fund:

- Removing capital export controls would stop Chinese individuals' savings suffering negative real interest rates of –3% with no alternative but expensive housing and probably overvalued local stocks.

- Investment abroad by Chinese individuals could be much more plausibly presented as genuine, spontaneous capital exports, justifying the current surplus that they offset – and with it, implicitly, the seemingly undervalued yuan. A sovereign investment fund is transparently a move to dispose of the proceeds of aggressive mercantilism.

- Capital flows overseas by private Chinese interests of any kind would reduce the monetary inflation involved in financing the accumulation of state-owned overseas assets.

- Withdrawal of funds by individuals from Chinese domestic bank accounts would raise interest rates, reducing the negative rates that sap current savings and dousing overheating domestic demand, especially excessive and wasteful capital spending.

• Longer-run consumer confidence could be desirably stimulated: the security offered by a far greater range of investment alternatives than the current dismal choices could strike at the roots of the savings glut. A shift from the glut of savings and investment to more conventional consumer satisfaction would be a clear sign of a more mature economy.

• Opening a 'window' at the People's Bank of China to hand out dollars at the current exchange rate (7.20 yuan to the dollar) would help fund the recapitalisation of the banks that might become necessary with an open capital account (or, the least, provision of liquidity in certain cases).

In August 2007, SAFE (the State Agency for Foreign Exchange) announced a tentative move in this direction, involving investment of funds in Hong Kong only. It was a half-baked proposal – better designed to provide plenty of 'fees' to communist officials and their Hong Kong associates than to free the operation of the economy. It also ignored the role of banking and securities regulators, who, not having been consulted, predictably came out in opposition. So: two steps forward, two steps back. But the idea has such major advantages that it seems likely to be revived in some form. An adaptation of the existing rules for overseas investment by 'qualified domestic institutional investor funds' could achieve most of what is needed, though probably with greater 'fee friction'.

No doubt any moves will be structured to provide a significant diversion of value to officialdom and its private-sector pilot-fish – but a glance at the rich fee structures of global investment banking proves that fee friction does not prevent good business being done. Moves are bound to be partial and tentative to start with, but fears of the impact of a withdrawal of deposits in domestic Chinese banks – in favour of investment overseas – are likely to be allayed by quite modest 'ripples' in the event. The 'hidden hand' may not be a principle overtly accepted by the leaders of the Chinese Communist Party, but they have by now had plenty of experience of it serving them well. It is to be hoped they give it a chance in this instance.

An important background point is that the addition to the free-market world economy of 2½ billion people from China, India and other countries over the past 25 years has boosted values of existing capital assets, especially equities, shifted income from labour to profits, and created a demand for fresh spending on productive assets. But an implication of the savings glut – which in general implies deficient domestic demand in the savings-glut countries – is that productive investment has been less than might be expected from this logic. Instead, the flow of cash has ended up in the asset that is there already, and has always been there: real estate, ultimately land.

The likely future direction of the Asian glut reflects at least three factors:

- A new wariness in China and elsewhere towards 'base load' lending to the money markets, evidenced by the higher spreads between Libor and both Treasury bills and central bank policy rates.

- Overvaluation of housing and real estate in the United States and Britain, with overbuilding the chief problem in Spain – for a while, prices are likely to decline.
- Enthusiasm for stocks in the Chinese private sector (households and business) with reduction of capital-export barriers between this demand and global stockmarkets

The effects could be impressive, even with US and European corporate profits falling over the next year or two as their economies slow. But any shift of the capital flow into equities is subject to major provisos about Chinese economic policies outlined above. An example illustrates the bullish argument. Suppose the long-run real return on US equities is 7% (as it has averaged 6¾% for the S&P since 1871). Then deducting 3% for real growth leaves a required dividend (or free-cash-flow) yield of 4%. With typical 'dividend cover' of 1½ times earnings (to finance asset build-up and provide growth), the earnings yield required is 6%. This inverts to a p/e ratio of 17 (100/6) which is – not by coincidence – the long-run average p/e ratio in the US market.

Now consider Chinese households or business savings as the marginal investor. Their baseline is bank deposits yielding –3%. They would probably happily accept a real yield on stocks below the long-run US average of 7%. Suppose they would settle for 5%. Then deduct 3% growth and the required free-cash-flow yield is 2%. Dividend cover of 1½ takes this up to an earnings yield of 3%: that is (inverted) a p/e ratio of 33 (100/3). This is twice the p/e ratio in the long-run average example. It would accommodate quite a large potential drop in earnings in the forthcoming US slowdown, to say the least. This example is not a forecast. It is an illustration of how Chinese money could transform global equity markets after the current hard landing has played itself out.

Will the Eurasian savings glut finally ease?

The qualified optimism about how the savings glut might be compatible with recovery is the principal issue for the recovery in the aftermath of 2008's likely world slowdown. Over a five-year timespan, however, global imbalances could be significantly reduced, even though they are probably still increasing at the start of 2008. To see how, or why, the basic causes of the savings glut must be reiterated (for more details, see the Appendix, pages 117–29):

- **Demographics: Japan and north-central Europe.** Slower growth or actual decline in population (and the 16–64 working-age cohort) reduces the need for construction and boosts savings once the 'baby-boomer' bulge retires.
- **Restructuring: Japan and north-central Europe.** Excessive debt and labour costs in Japan (mid-1990s) and north-central Europe (especially Germany after reunification and EMU) caused drastic cost cutting to boost business cash flow and remedy excessive debt.
- **Primitive financial systems and social security: developing Asia.** The lack of assured provision for job loss or ill health, or for ageing, together with undeveloped mortgage markets, forces much higher personal savings rates.
- **Mercantilist export-led growth: developing Asia.** Proven efficacy

of export-led growth caused development strategies leading to surplus.

• **Shock effect of Asian crisis: developing Asia.** Slippage into mid-1990s deficits after an inflationary boom, with weak financial systems, resulted in a massive regional crisis that made authorities say 'never again'. Result: surpluses and build-up of foreign-exchange reserves.

The emphasis in this book has been on the near-explosive Chinese surplus. But we have seen how Japan's policy has also raised its surplus steadily. North-central Europe has prospered in the recent world boom: Germany, with half the north-central Europe countries' GDP, had a 2007 surplus of $200 billion (6% of GDP); but the other north-central Europe countries' surpluses are relatively larger, for example the Netherlands (7% of GDP), Sweden (7%), Switzerland (16%) and Norway (15%), the last admittedly a major oil exporter. The Asian Tigers have modestly rising surpluses owing to the world boom. (In contrast with the Appendix, Russia has been treated here as an oil exporter, though it continues to be in structural surplus, unlikely to be eliminated soon, whereas OPEC's probably will be.)

The Eurasian savings glut could be on the cusp and may soon decline, perhaps quite rapidly. In Japan, the original savings-glut country, it would already be falling fast if fiscal policy was less tight. The private net savings surplus (gross savings minus capital formation) at its peak in 2002–03 was over 11% of GDP. This was mostly offset by a government budget deficit of 8%, only 3% being the overseas surplus. But the budget deficit was already down to 2½% of GDP in 2006. In 2007 it is likely to have been eliminated, possibly replaced by a surplus, so severe has been fiscal austerity. This could well be the signal for the Ministry of Finance to ease its fiscal stance. In that case the strong finances of the private sector, the combination of very low interest rates and reasonably priced housing, and the diminishing need for a retiring population to save, could quickly revive domestic demand. If and when that happens, the yen would rise fast and the surplus would shrink.

In non-Chinese Asian Tigers, similar trends to those suggested for Japan are already in place. Budgets and policy generally were kept very tight in the early 2000s after the shock of the Asian crisis. But confidence is now stronger, and a weakening in export markets in 2008 could well be the signal for some counter-cyclical easing of fiscal and monetary policy. For example, in South Korea, the largest, the budget *surplus* is 3% of GDP.

In China, with exports still on a 25% growth path versus 20% for imports, it is too early to suggest the surplus is topping out. If the yuan appreciates more sharply in future, the first effect – before discouragement of export volume and encouragement of import volume kick in – will be to widen the surplus somewhat: in dollar terms, a higher yuan could raise export values while leaving imports unchanged. But over the next few years, imports could surge as domestic demand continues to grow, while a rising yuan makes them cheaper. Combined with slower growth in export markets and some erosion of cost-competitiveness, this could eventually put the Chinese surplus into reverse, though it is likely to fall back only slowly.

In Europe, the rising euro is combining with prospective weakness not only in the United States but also in important peripheral European countries – Britain, Spain, Italy and Ireland – to sap the future surpluses in north-central Europe. In a 2008–09 downswing, fiscal stimulation (north-central Europe has budgets in balance or surplus) could add to domestic demand and imports. In the medium term, the retirement of baby-boomers and the lesser need for drastic business restructuring should lower the savings rate of households and businesses, respectively, providing a sustained upward push to demand.

Indeed, it is not impossible to envisage – 5–10 years hence – deficits in Europe and a swing to balance or even surplus in America. The trends mentioned above should deplete the structural north-central European surplus and mean a western European deficit given the red ink in the other countries. But American baby-boomers are going to reach 65 and find that their pension 'pot' is empty or inadequate, and the hoped-for sale of the big house to downsize on retirement is thwarted by the housing debacle. (Major housing downswings generally last five years.) They will have to carry on working until 70, saving hard to build up pension provisions. US GDP would be driven by exports, with domestic demand restrained by higher savings and the dollar competitively cheap. My colleague Gabriel Stein has entertainingly outlined this scenario in a Lombard Street Research *Monthly Review* (no. 204, August 2006, 'The coming US current account surplus and other stories').

These possibilities do not remove the need for equity flows to render the Eurasian savings glut constructive and sustainable for the next few years, but they may reduce the duration of the 'gobbling up' of US equities that appears to be causing alarm in some quarters.

Crucial policy decisions: enlightenment or blunders?

So what will happen to Chinese flows, and how readily will they benefit stocks? These are the policy conditions on global optimism mentioned above – with the primary role reserved for Beijing. The principal issues are relaxation of capital export controls and demand management policy. Taking the latter first, the crucial change during 2007 was that China's GDP growth took its level above its trend, into overheating, for the first time since 2000. Suddenly, the huge annual gains in exports are no longer an unambiguous advantage to China.

The Chinese government has three options in the immediate term – accept inflation, deflate domestic demand, or let the yuan appreciate radically (see page 17) – and the last option is the only rational choice. The impact could be softened, in terms of the pace of rebalancing the economy, by liberating capital exports by individuals, with all the advantages mentioned on pages 87–8. If these two policies were implemented – with a due respect for gradualism in adjusting major strategies – most of the risk of the Asian savings glut would leach away. The short-term downswing in the United States and (to a lesser extent Europe) would by no means be obviated, but a clear path to recovery would exist. For example, if the US stockmarket and private company value of $20 trillion were to grow at a nominal 5% (2½% each for real GDP and prices) its increment each year would be $1 trillion. Foreign investors could pick up $500 billion of this in equity capital inflows to finance the deficit, still leaving some growth for existing investors. Over a very long time, this process could become unacceptable, but as we have seen, the durability of these huge Eurasian structural surpluses may not be as apparently unlimited as it was two years ago.

If China's economy is brought under control purely by cutting into domestic demand, with inflation meanwhile accelerating to around 10%, the government will be maximising its unpopularity at home and the hostility of both the West and its neighbours in the region. Unlikely a course though this may seem, it does represent the path of least resistance, that is inertia, or habit. The cheap yuan mercantilist policy has served China well, and there will be influential voices in the government opposing any change. As for relaxing controls on exports of capital, old communist objections to loss of control over citizens could reinforce fears about withdrawal of cash from Chinese banks leading to financial instability. It is from such quarters that resistance to change is likely. But clearly the pain of staying with current policies is likely to increase – which should diminish resistance to change.

Much hangs on this. Failure to check exports – that is, deeper western market penetration worsening the pain of a slowdown – could provoke trade retaliation, especially in Europe where the problem is most acute, give the US pursuit of blatant competitive dollar depreciation (with China covertly following in its footsteps). At this point, a serious European consensus in favour of import restrictions is unlikely. The problem would be if China is prepared to respond only to a serious European threat, by which time the process of assembling European consensus in favour of action may make it unstoppable.

When it comes to countries willingly accepting Chinese equity inroads – as was done with Japanese flows in the late 1980s and early 1990s – the difficulties seem less dangerous. To be sure, the United States might adopt a nationalistic approach – it already has heavy and absurd restrictions on foreign ownership of airlines and media companies, for example. But the Chinese funds would simply go elsewhere: arbitrage between different equity markets would then take care of much of the required onward flow, though US real incomes would meanwhile be lowered by a negative relative wealth effect. As it is the United States that is likely to remain in deficit for several years, it would simply have to maintain a lower exchange rate, with slower consumption and faster net export growth than if it accepted Chinese equity inflows. This would be a limited, local US problem, with little effect on the world economy.

So the key policy decisions for a reasonable medium-term recovery from the likely global economic downswing will be made in China. But for the rest of the world it will be important to maintain the free-market trade and capital-flow policies that have nurtured globalisation and created mass western and Asian wealth over the past 25 years.

APPENDIX

THE BILL FROM
THE CHINA SHOP

HOW ASIA'S SAVINGS GLUT THREATENS
THE WORLD ECONOMY

Charles Dumas

(Essay first published in March 2006;
charts updated to end 2007)

Contents

Figures and tables

Acknowledgements

The specific idea of inverting global imbalances from a US deficit problem to a Eurasian surplus problem was mine, but it owed a lot to the *zeitgeist* in 2004, with the dollar growing ever weaker and no sign of any improvement in the US deficit. The growing importance of China was also widely appreciated.

The Chinese yuan–dollar peg was constantly discussed with Brian Reading and other colleagues at Lombard Street Research. Brian contributed much of the structural thinking behind the concept of the New Dollar Area, the quasi-fixed, trans-Pacific currency zone made up of the US, China, Japan and the Asian Tigers. The determined sustenance of Asian surpluses involved in such exchange-rate policies was a key factor pointing to structural surpluses, rather than merely investor preferences for US securities, as the fundamental reason for US deficits being so easily financed. Some of these issues had also come up in a presentation by Martin Wolf of the *Financial Times* to the Political Economy Club. The use of sectoral financial balances – analysis of the interactive financial balances and behaviour patterns of households, businesses, the government and the rest of the world – was pioneered by Brian thirty years ago, and has been vital to our approach. I owe him a lot.

The thought that there should be an actual book came from

Frank Veneroso, who played a large part in Lombard Street Research's New York seminar on the Eurasian surpluses and Chinese slowdown, held on 8 March 2005, a fortuitous two days before Ben Bernanke's speech talking of a 'global savings glut'.

Our colleagues in Lombard Street Research have been models of patience as the work on this book has sometimes distracted us from full attention to our duties. Peter Allen, our managing director, has also been instrumental in securing its publication, whipping us on, and helping with editing, the title, the cover illustration, and numerous other important aspects of the fact that it is here at all.

Introduction

Most of us are influenced by Mr Micawber's dictum: 'Annual income twenty pounds, annual expenditure nineteen nineteen six, result happiness. Annual income twenty pounds, annual expenditure twenty pounds ought and six, result misery.' Translation: deficits are bad, surpluses are good. It is a natural viewpoint that the purpose of politics and policy is to put right wrongs. So, even if we cannot create happiness, let us at least attack misery! Away, deficits and borrowing!

We are also in the habit of regarding the United States as active, others as reactive. America has the largest and most persistent deficits. So US deficits are the cause of the global financial imbalances. Right?

Wrong!

The world has an Asian current-account surplus problem rather than a US current-account deficit problem. The complex effects of this surplus have been central to our analysis of the world economy since mid-2004 and underpin the argument of this book. After five or six years of accepting consensus views about the 'unsustainable' US deficit(s), the fact that they were nevertheless sustained began to force a rethink. Hence the idea that they are not some peculiar perversion, but are derived from something more fundamental and structural – an effect, not a cause. In March 2005, Ben Bernanke, successor to Alan Greenspan as chairman of the Federal Reserve, followed the same logic, attributing US financial deficits to an 'Asian savings glut'. For the Fed, his argument is convenient almost to the point of being self-serving. But it seems right.[1]

This book sets out the concept of the Eurasian savings excess as a structural rather than cyclical phenomenon. Although north-central Europe has a large portion of the Eurasian structural surplus, by late 2005 it was almost entirely offset by deficits elsewhere in Europe. So the story breaks down into an intra-European imbalance and a global imbalance, the latter almost entirely driven by the Asian savings glut, which is therefore the phrase mostly used here. It describes the 'perfect storm' comprising four largely unrelated forces, and the countries to which they variously apply. It examines how the start of this structural surplus manifested itself in the US 1998–2000 bubble.

The alternative responses by policymakers and the private sector are outlined. The surplus tends to inflate asset prices, but not consumer prices – the 'Goldilocks' economy – so long as global demand is sustained by deficit policies. The post-bubble recovery in 2002–05 is shown to depend on spectacularly easy fiscal and monetary policies, and the consequent build-up of household debt; both of these in any other circumstances would quickly have caused major inflation. The new dollar area with its semi-fixed exchange rates has been a key transmission mechanism for the Asian glut. This is based on the Chinese yuan–dollar peg: other Asian countries have managed their exchange rates in order to match the yuan out of fear of being 'hollowed out' by China's burgeoning manufacturing prowess. After a look at the long-term damage from savings excesses in Japan (1990–2003) the title essay of the book concludes with the stresses that threaten this Sino-US synergy of lending and borrowing, and hence global growth. A severe trans-Pacific crisis is forecast for 2007.

1

Typhoon surplus

Economics is a combination of, and a balancing act between, science and art. Scientific propositions such as Newton's Third Law of Motion – 'To every action there is an equal and opposite reaction' – have their counterparts. For every borrower there is a lender, and vice versa. At the macro-level, for every deficit there is a surplus, and vice versa. These two propositions are closer to being self-evident than even Newton's Third Law. The art of economics, by contrast, comes in the many instances where judgement is required, as well as an understanding of laws and theory. An example is deciding, in the case of borrowing and lending, which is the cause and which is the effect, assuming this can be done. (Interactive cause and effect is also often observed.) In monetary theory, it is usual to see borrowing as the action and lending as the reaction. In a closed economy (one with no external sector, neither foreign trade nor capital flows) to have it the other way round would be strange. But it is not conceptually impossible.

Although the world as a whole is a closed economy, individual countries are not. But we are accustomed to see deficits (borrowing)

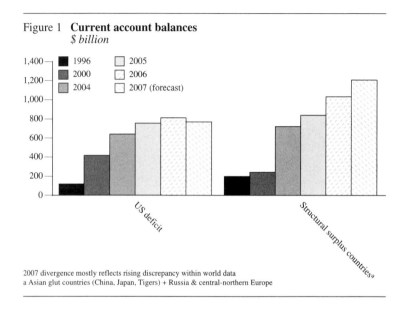

Figure 1 **Current account balances**
$ billion

2007 divergence mostly reflects rising discrepancy within world data
a Asian glut countries (China, Japan, Tigers) + Russia & central-northern Europe

as the action, and the equal and opposite surpluses (lending) as
the reaction. This is true both between open economies in the
world at large, and within economies (closed or open) between
borrowers and lenders.

This book is intended to expose these misconceptions. It is the
Asian current-account surpluses that are the fundamental driver,
as large and chronic surpluses in central-northern Europe are to
a great degree offset by deficits elsewhere within Europe. The
US deficit is the reaction – not so much profligate extravagance,
but the result of pursuing full-employment/low-inflation policies
in a world full of countries determined to run surpluses. This is
not an iron-clad, bullet-proof assertion. Elements of fiscal and
monetary irresponsibility can be found in US policies over the

past five or six years, it must be said, but the broad direction of causation is clear. Asian (and some European) countries run high-savings/current-account surplus economies partly as a matter of policy and partly for deep structural and behavioural reasons. America and to a lesser degree Britain and Australia (and now European countries such as Italy, Spain and increasingly France) have simply adjusted their fiscal and monetary policies to borrow Asia's excess savings. It would be rude to refuse!

In this interpretation of recent events, the one 'problem' that does not exist is the US trade or current deficit (now nearly $800 billion a year). The problem is not for the United States to find $2 billion a day to fund its deficit, as has so often been stated. Rather, the problem is for the Asian, together with some European, countries to find a home for $1.5 billion a day of capital generated by their surpluses. This surplus moves like a tidal wave from balance sheet to balance sheet, between businesses, households and government, loading them with extra debt. It has helped induce undue borrowing by US business (1998–2000), by Australian and British households (1999–2004), by American households (2001–05), by Chinese business (2002–04) and recently by Spain and increasingly Italy.

Asia's decisive shift into current-account surplus came after the 1997–98 Asian crisis. Initially, the surplus typhoon strongly reinforced the Wall Street bubble of 1998–2000; then it drove the British and Australian debt-fuelled housing booms of 1999–2004. Both countries developed large, easily financed deficits during this period. American households followed suit from late 2001, and Asian surpluses were recycled back into a Chinese boom in 2002–04. To this private-sector debt stimulation must be added acceptance in the United States, Europe and Japan of government deficits far beyond what is generally regarded as prudent – especially in the context of looming pension financing problems in most of these countries. The exhaustion of borrowing power in private-sector balance sheets is now increasingly likely – and soon – after which persistent Asian surpluses are likely to cause a general global deflation. Government deficits worldwide will further expand. How governments handle their fast-growing indebtedness to surplus nations alongside financing baby-boomers' pensions will be the western nations' economic challenge of the next 5–10 years.

What does 'excessive saving' mean?

Current-account surpluses represent the excess of a country's domestic savings over its investment. Globally, they must be matched by deficits elsewhere (though in practice because of measurement errors there is always a trivial difference). Put another way, the world's saving and investment have to be equal. Saving equals income minus consumption, government plus household. Investment equals output, i.e. GDP, which should equal income minus the part consumed. So saving equals investment by definition. But if the desire to invest is less than the desire to save, demand will fall short: unwanted investment in the form of stock – inventory – will occur, leading to a downward economic spiral if no other factor intervenes. (See Chapter 2 for

Table 1 **Swing in US and European budget deficits after the bubble**

| | Government balance (% GDP) | | Difference | |
	2000	2004	%	$ billion
US	1.6	–4.3	–5.9	690
Euro zone	0.1	–2.7	–2.8	270
UK	1.6	–3.4	–5.0	110
Total	1.0	–3.6	–4.6	1,070

Note. Japan's deficit was already 7.5% of GDP by 2000, as its problems dated from earlier; a small improvement to 6.1% in 2004 was offset by Scandinavian worsening.

other possible consequences of an excessive desire to save.) The idea proposed here of excessive Asian surpluses implies a global propensity to save that is greater than investment, unless lower interest rates or fiscal policy respond.

To reconcile this apparent contradiction in the concept of a savings glut is not difficult. First, recent years have seen a major growth in deficit countries – and some surplus countries – deliberately dis-saving by running government deficits. This offsets the rising structural saving in the surplus countries' private sectors (Japan and north-central Europe) and in developing countries in Asia. Second, what would threaten to be saving in excess of investment may induce more investment through the operation of depressed real rates of return. Initially, this means lower real bond yields. But as the 'wall of money' drives up stock and real estate prices, another result is lower earnings yields in stockmarkets (i.e. higher price/earnings ratios). Likewise rising property prices

Figure 2 **Overnight interbank money-market rates**
%

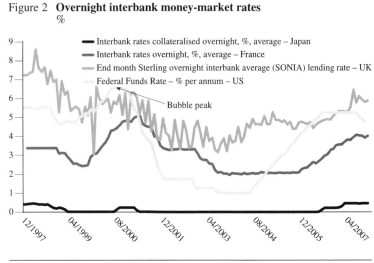

mean lower rental yields in real estate (with high capitalisation ratios).

So far, the primary effect of these lower real yields (apart from making existing wealth-holders much more wealthy) has not been to induce lower-return capital spending, except in the initial case of the US bubble and the more recent 2003–04 Chinese investment boom. Rather, deficit countries have induced lower household savings by easy monetary policies, in parallel with the government dis-saving from easy fiscal policies. The UK, Australian and US 'borrow-and-spend' household spending orgies of the past few years are the first result, reflecting easy monetary and fiscal policies, and easy access to excess Asian saving.

This aggressive cut in government and household saving has substantially exceeded the structural Asian and central-northern

Europe excess savings, and world savings have gone down a little. IMF calculations of world savings put them at 21.5% of the world's $40 trillion GDP in 2004, compared with 22% in 2000. So in four years, in which US-European government deficits rose by $1.1 trillion and US household deficits by a further $250 billion, the global savings rate fell by $200 billion or so (0.5% of $40 billion). This graphically shows the force of burgeoning savings. The chief danger from current-account deficits, most of all in America, arises from these internal cuts in savings, which are achieved by running up debt, rather than from external debt and deficit financing.

It is one thing to assert that America has no problem attracting $2 billion a day of capital inflows. It is quite another to contemplate the point that its recently depressed national savings rate of 14% of GDP will in due course have to be raised. The difference between this and the national investment rate of 20% of GDP mirrors the current-account deficit, which is 6–6.5% of GDP. Not only is investment only 60% covered by saving, but domestic demand is over 106% of GDP. As US GDP is close to its potential, this gap can only be narrowed – if it is to be narrowed – by cuts in domestic demand. Although the structural nature of the Asian surpluses means this problem will probably not be forced to resolution by US creditors, the time of reckoning will come – soon if the argument in the last section of this book is correct. But American consumers undoubtedly regard this overconsumption as their entitlement. When the punch-bowl is taken away, the end of the party, and the relapse into hangover, could prove ugly.

Another, deeper, aspect of this excess of savings is the wasted

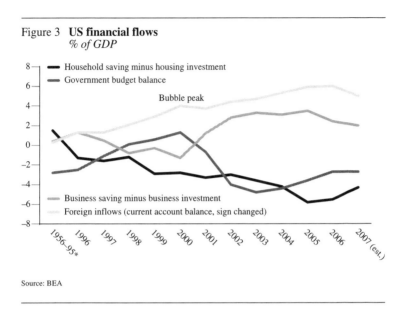

Figure 3 **US financial flows**
% of GDP

- Household saving minus housing investment
- Government budget balance
- Business saving minus business investment
- Foreign inflows (current account balance, sign changed)

Bubble peak

Source: BEA

opportunity it represents. One way to look at the world economy today is to say that a relatively balanced OECD economy in the late 1980s – with capital and labour reasonably in proportion to one another – has been destabilised by entry of the former Soviet bloc and, more importantly, some 1.25 billion Chinese and 1 billion Indians. Among other effects, the bargaining power of western labour is reduced, alongside the capital assets per potential worker. This has been tough on low-income labour in rich countries. It has also underpinned the huge gains in value of existing capital assets (stocks and real estate). High-income labour as well as wealth-holders in rich countries have benefited from these gains.

One result should be a massive investment boom in response to such high returns on assets – a boom that would provide China,

India and eastern European countries with capital assets, transferring technology and raising their average incomes. To some extent this has happened. But major blockages have slowed development – which is tragic, because but for these blockages there would be plenty of highly profitable usages for all the savings the world could muster, and no Asian savings glut. Western countries and governments would not need to induce deficits to dissipate these savings in 'borrow-and-spend'.

The obstructions to adequate growth in the former Soviet bloc are too complex to detail here (and at their worst in eastern Germany). In China, the government's control of both the energy sector (with price controls as well) and the financial sector, and fundamental conditions in the housing sector, together with general problems of corruption and the rule of law, severely hobble growth. Impressive though it is with an annual trend of 8–9%, it should be 11–12%. India, as well as being restricted by appalling infrastructure, has restrictive labour laws that hold back the manufacturing sector and many services. These have ensured that the country with the poorest workers on earth has extremely capital-intensive rather than labour-intensive growth. Ten-year average GDP growth has accelerated to 6.25%, but it should (given other factors) be close to 10%.[2]

The Asian savings glut

A key point is that Asian excess savings are structural, not cyclical. This analysis does not draw conclusions from the essentially cyclical OPEC and Canadian surpluses, which could dissipate quite quickly through some combination of oil prices falling, rapid increases in imports, or (especially for Canada) real exchange-rate rises. Better trade balances in Latin America and elsewhere, based on the strength of the global economy (and helped by hefty devaluations quite recently), are likewise not the issue. The contention that US current-account deficits are largely the result of Asian surpluses can only justify sustained fiscal and monetary ease if those surpluses are regarded as structural for the medium term.

Different forces in different countries lead to this common result of persistent current-account surpluses. In China and the Asian Tigers (South Korea, Taiwan, Hong Kong, Thailand, Malaysia, Singapore and Indonesia), development strategy and policy are crucial. Export-led development, the Asian approach, naturally tends to lead to exports surpluses, though they are not inevitable. In developing Asia, where strong exports are buttressed by high savings, a surplus is likely. Moreover, although it is effective to focus development policy on exports, that leaves the domestic financial system crudely devoted to industry, and undeveloped in provision for household needs. This results in high savings rates as financial products for house purchase (mortgages), health and pension provision (insurance and fund management) are neglected. The absence of public social security as well as sophisticated private financial products requires people to save much more to take care of basic realities: losing your job or your health, getting old, buying a house, and so on.

Savings in an economy can be made by households (easily

understood, if complex statistically) or by business, with government budget balances also affecting the overall national savings rate. Business savings are its cash flow matching depreciation (of existing equipment) plus the retained profit that remains after paying interest, taxes and dividends. The structural excess saving in the developed world arises partly from business 'restructuring' – saving much more than is needed for capital spending. The other chief driving force is demography: declining working-age (and increasingly total) populations need less construction investment in particular, as existing factories and offices are sufficient. Large pre-retirement populations can also mean high personal savings rates, as people anticipate post-retirement financial needs. In Japan, business-sector restructuring now predominates as the source of high private-sector saving. But 10–15 years ago excessive Japanese saving was chiefly the result of demography, which remains important. In Germany, Benelux, Scandinavia and Switzerland ('north-central Europe') demography has predominated, but business restructuring is increasingly a factor.

Business restructuring (leading to financial surpluses) has also been significant in the US since the bubble burst in 2000. In overall terms, financial flows must add up to zero – as we saw, each surplus must correspond to somebody else's deficit, and vice versa. So to the US current-account deficit, also known as foreigners' surplus, must be added a business surplus. Only the government and households remain to run the corresponding deficits. So the US business surpluses mean these balancing domestic government and household deficits are even larger than the external deficit that matches other countries' surpluses.

In a global sense, the saving glut is a good example of that fashionable concept, the 'perfect storm'. The mercantilist, market-predatory, export-led policies of Asian developing countries may have greater impact relative to world GDP than similar behaviour in the heyday of Japan (1960s) or South Korea (1970s). But by themselves they could probably be accommodated, along with the structural tendency towards high household savings in countries pursuing the Asian growth model. The natural tendency towards financial surplus in the late careers of 'baby-boomers', exaggerated by fears of ageing arising from rapidly growing longevity, ought to be offset by the capital spending requirements of fast growth in America and rapid development in the emerging markets. But the latter is thwarted by domestic development policy weaknesses as well as the Asian export-led, high-savings model.

The possibility of simply expanding business investment to use up the spare capital is quite rightly rejected by western businesses themselves. They have learned the lessons of the US bubble in 1998–2000 and the Japanese bubble of the late 1980s. This reinforces the shift to shareholder value from bureaucratic business waste, originated by fear of Carl Icahn, T. Boone Pickens and the other corporate raiders of the 1980s, financed by Mike Milken's junk bonds. Rather than being taken over and restructured to generate cash flow and pay off a mound of junk debt, US businesses decided to do the job themselves (keeping their own jobs in the process). Restructuring spread round the world (with a lapse in the bubble), and now worldwide business restructuring is the fourth element of this perfect storm of urge to surplus.

China and the Asian Tigers

Strong growth in China and the Asian Tigers, where open-economy, export-led, high-savings policies have been adopted, contrasts starkly with dismal results in Latin America and pre-1980s India, where low savings, capital imports and import-substitution created closed, siege economies. In Latin America, any move into rapid growth naturally gave rise to booming capital spending – inevitably, given major catch-up potential. With feeble domestic savings, such bursts of growth therefore required soaring imports, not just for financial reasons (i.e. lack of domestic savings) but also for lack of competitive domestic capital goods industries (except perhaps construction). Such growth periods were therefore quickly choked off by debt crises as foreign lenders were discouraged by inflation and deficits, soon followed by inability or unwillingness to repay.

The import-substitution, siege-economy mentality also entailed obstacles to foreign direct investment, such as domestic content quotas, dividend restraints, etc. Meanwhile, competitiveness was further thwarted by domestic cliques and cartels carving up the protected local market. And developing a wide range of industries on a small scale to supply the local market means forgoing the economies of scale that can result from focusing on a few well-chosen export industries. India remained financially sound, but simply grew consistently too slowly until the 1980s, with similar constraints.

The Pacific Rim countries' mercantilist approach has ensured competitive industries, because of the need to compete in export

Figure 4 **Actual exports plus imports**
% of GDP, divided by predicted ratio based on population

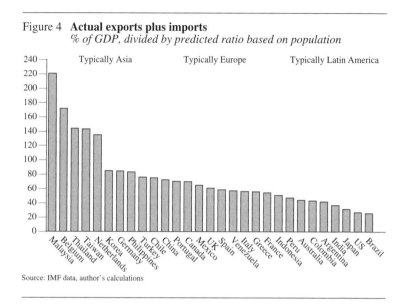

Source: IMF data, author's calculations

markets, and has tended to promote economies of scale. With high savings as well as export focus, capital investment needs, and the imports to supply them, have been easily financed not merely without incurring foreign debt, but with a surplus too. In fact, capital inflows have added to the surplus requiring a 'home' abroad: while the treatment of foreign capital has certainly not been uniformly free-market and transparent, China and others have encouraged direct investment to good effect in achieving rapid technology transfer and job creation.

So far, so good. But Asian fixation on exports and revulsion from deficits became more profound as a result of the inflationary boom–bust of China in 1993–94 and, especially, the Asian crisis of 1997–98. Humiliation was heaped on Asian countries, as their underdeveloped financial systems collapsed under the huge inflows, followed by outflows, of global finance in the 1995–98 boom–bust. This transformed attitudes towards free capital flows. IMF policies towards South Korea and others were clearly driven more by western bank and hedge fund interests than the countries' development needs. 'Never again' has entered the Asian policy vocabulary, in China as much as the countries most affected. The resulting policies – and surpluses – have been and probably will remain persistent.

Japan

The source of surpluses is quite different in Japan. Demographic factors may have held up household savings rates in the 1990s, when the large 1930s generation was in its pre-retirement phase, but now they have retired, personal savings are well below European levels (relative to income) though still well above America's near-zero. It is business that contributes nearly 25 points of Japan's 29% of GDP private-sector savings rate. But private investment needs are less than this by at least 10% of GDP. Here, demographic factors remain important: both the slow growth trend of 2% or less – cutting the need for business investment – and the weakness of house-building have a lot to do with the shrinking working-age population. Private investment is unlikely to raise its share of GDP in future, and could decrease it. So the private sector (unless the economy is to slump) has to run a surplus (be a net lender) of 10% of GDP. Japan's current recovery, including rising house prices for the first time for 15 years, may reduce this surplus over time. Personal savings could be cut by a rundown of huge bank deposits held by some people as a cushion against formerly increasing negative housing equity, and by others as a vehicle for pension provision. As the population ages, having had little or nothing in the late 1940s, it could well consume some of its now large wealth. But such a development is uncertain and likely to be slow.

Once again: for every surplus (lender) there is an equal and opposite deficit (borrower). Apart from the private sector, Japan has only government and foreigners as potential borrowers (i.e. sources of offsetting deficits). For Japan to be close to full employment, government deficits plus current-account surpluses (i.e. foreigners' borrowing) must add up to 10% of GDP. Not surprisingly, it wants as large a current-account surplus as possible to reduce reliance on what is already an alarming build-up of government debt. (In 2004, for example, while the current-account surplus was 3.5% of GDP, the government deficit was 6.5%.) Although the huge 10% private-sector savings surplus should eventually dissipate, businesses still have a way to go to get debt and assets down to stable long-term levels after the excesses of Japan's late-1980s bubble, followed by the delay of business restructuring until 1997 and after. So the country's surplus with the rest of the world is unlikely to ease much in the next three years or so. Japan's private savings of $1.1 trillion are three-quarters of those in the United States, though its economy is less than two-fifths the size. Its excessive savings are a major global force.

Russia

The oligarchs who own much of Russian business effectively stole it in the 1990s. Typically, a new owner, having paid little for business assets in a corrupt privatisation, would generate cash in the company by not paying the wages. The resulting cash would be parked in a Swiss bank account and then transferred into the personal account of the oligarch. So the very process of stealing the money involved capital exports. President Vladimir Putin came to power on a populist wave at least partly because of this. His imprisonment of Mikhail Khodorkovsky, the head of oil giant Yukos, has put the oligarchs on notice. Their natural reactions include continuing to export as much capital as they can (along with their families). Russia's gross savings rate is 31% of GDP, the investment rate is 21%, leaving a current-account surplus of a whopping 10%, some $60 billion.

Russia's chief source of export revenue, as well as oligarchs' wealth, is oil and gas, so the world boom is swelling surpluses in a purely cyclical way. Unlike the structural excess savings, which are inherently linked to a deficiency of demand, cyclical oil-exporting surpluses reflect excess demand, and exacerbate it as the revenues are spent on imports. This concentration of the increased global financial imbalances this year on oil exporters, i.e. cyclical factors reflecting excess demand, is a development that could hasten the debt problems that are likely to end this world boom prematurely. This is discussed more fully in the last section of this book, but it downplays the importance of the Russian surplus in a discussion of a savings glut.

North-central Europe

Germany – and much of north-central Europe – has a large structural surplus, mostly for demographic reasons. Fearful that extravagant state pension promises will be broken, baby-boomers – who have between 6 and 24 years to go before they are 65 – are saving more. In Germany, on the spending side, after five decades of heavy building culminating in the post-reunification boom of 1990–94, a shrinking working-age population means few more (if any) factories or office buildings will ever be needed. The future contraction soon expected for the total population (i.e. not just working-age) may soon make this true of homes too. Yet the construction share of German GDP is still close to that of the United States, despite ten years of shrinkage since the 1994 peak. By now construction should be minimal; its downswing has therefore a lot further to go.

Meanwhile, the recent surge of German business restructuring – i.e. cost-cutting – and the resulting erosion of job security contributes further to households' urge to save, as well as raising savings directly via unspent business cash flow. Similar if lesser forces are at work in Benelux, Scandinavia and Switzerland. The combined personal and business savings add up to a private savings rate of 23% of GDP, and rising, for these countries together. This is far ahead of investment in business and housing – the difference creates a private-sector financial surplus. Though partly offset by government dis-saving of more than 1% of GDP in Germany, this surplus has no such outlet in Benelux, Scandinavia and Switzerland, which are mostly models of fiscal rectitude. So it expresses itself in a huge current surplus. As the rising euro in 2002–04 cut European export competitiveness, deficient demand also resulted, lowering incomes (and therefore savings as well).

The impact of north-central Europe's excess savings is softened outside Europe not only by deficits in Mediterranean Europe (including now France), but also in Britain and the former communist countries of eastern Europe. Thus the massive north-central current surplus of $250 billion in 2004 was reduced by $80 billion of net combined deficit in France (only slight in 2004, though larger in 2005), Spain, Italy, Portugal and Greece, and by a further $50 billion of UK current deficit. The resulting western European surplus was $120 billion. As this includes the dampening effect of weak domestic demand on income and savings, it can be considered the structural contribution of Europe to the global structural surplus. Some of it was absorbed by eastern European countries' deficits, but nearly $100 billion has to be pooled into the global problem, which is mostly played out in Asian-US trade and capital flows. (This number would be much larger without the much criticised government deficits in countries such as Germany, France, Italy and Britain.)

During 2005, the north-central European surpluses changed little – despite higher oil costs – but rapid demand growth in the Mediterranean countries and eastern Europe has sharply increased their deficits, virtually eliminating the European element in the global surplus glut. Instead a rapidly worsening imbalance within Europe itself has developed, with alarming implications for the durability of some Mediterranean countries' membership of the monetary union.

The 2004 current surpluses of the countries considered here – using the western European surplus of $120 billion as its contribution to the problem – totalled $500 billion (see Figure 1). Although this does not account for the full US current deficit of $670 billion that year (close to $800 billion in 2005), adding in the OPEC surplus and taking account of the cyclical surpluses in Canada and Latin America more than takes care of the difference. In other words, about three-quarters of the US deficit was structural, 'using up' these structural surpluses. The other quarter was trivial on a world scale. The structural element in this surplus redistributed itself during 2005 – sharply up in China, down in Europe – while the US deficit grew larger for cyclical reasons (offset by larger oil exporters' surpluses). But although a strong US downswing could – indeed, on the forecasts here is likely to – cut oil exporters' surpluses, cutting the structural Asian surplus will require either a drastic global recession or major policy changes that may only be achievable through western pressure.

While the structural surpluses are the chief manifestations of financial imbalance, they are the tip of the iceberg: below the surface lies the scale of savings relative to the capital needs of the economy. The savings data are the bedrock of this analysis, and the justification for Mr Bernanke's talk of an 'Asian savings glut'. US national savings were less than 14% of GDP in 2004, at just over $1.6 trillion. They have in effect been 'crowded out' over several years by surpluses flowing in from abroad. The national savings of China alone were more than half this in dollar terms, on a GDP only one-seventh of that of the United States. China's national savings rate was a staggering half of GDP in 2004.

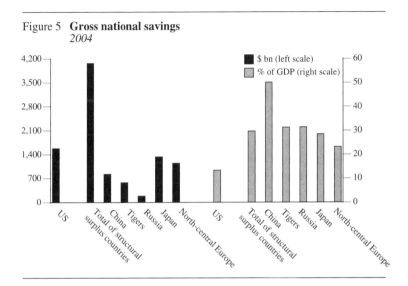

Figure 5 **Gross national savings**
          2004

China and the Asian Tigers had savings of $1.45 trillion, Japan had $1.33 trillion of private-sector savings, and the north-central European countries' private savings were $1.14 trillion. Even Russia's savings were $180 billion. The total of these savings was over $4 trillion, two and a half times US savings. The ratio of this $4 trillion to their combined GDP of $13.7 trillion (less than 20% above the United States) was 30%, more than twice America's 14%. This excessive desire for surpluses and savings is the root cause of global financial imbalances.

2

Excess savings:
alternative effects and responses

An excessive propensity to save in a group of countries, as described here, can lead to only a limited variety of effects or responses:

1 **Higher private investment.** For investment to be higher than it would be otherwise, and use up the excess saving, the required rate of return on new assets has to be driven down. Such a lower rate of return would be a natural thing to expect if the supply of funds (saving) is boosted. In pre-Keynesian, classical economics, this is the normal, orthodox response.

2 **Lower private savings.** Without any changes in public policy, a lower rate of return might also (on reasonable though not invariably correct assumptions) be expected to lessen the attraction of private saving, whether in the glut countries or (more likely) elsewhere. Again this is a natural classical response.

3 **Easier monetary policy.** Easier money in non-glut countries

could use up excess savings in a number of ways. First, by validating and promoting a lower rate of interest (the fundamental cost of capital) it could induce a combination of higher investment and lower savings, provoking via policy the two responses already described. Second, where an economy is below full employment (whether or not caused by the savings glut) it could induce growth in domestic demand and net imports.

4 Easier fiscal policy. The government can directly dis-save or invest, offsetting the savings glut, by shifting towards deficit financing. (This was Keynes's last-resort remedy in the Depression, and Keynesians' first-resort remedy for any slowdown since 1945.)

5 Depression of demand, income and output. If none of the above occurs on sufficient scale, the potential savings glut will express itself as deficient demand, lowering output and incomes to the level where the saving out of such income is no longer higher than investment. The investment in such scenarios generally includes a large measure of unwanted inventory, as sales fall short of businesses' expectations. This inventory hangover lowers future demand – i.e. raises further the potential savings surplus. Demand, income and output enter a downward spiral.

The story here is of how various combinations of the first four responses, in various countries, have enabled the fifth, Depression, to be avoided – and of how a major risk of Depression, or liquidity trap, still exists. The story has already been suggested in the analysis of the meaning of 'excessive saving' (the propensity to save, so-called ex-ante saving): i.e. the savings people and businesses desire to save ahead of the event, rather than what they are actually able to save in the event. This ex-ante savings rate cannot be directly measured, as saving is only known after the event, ex post. As measured after the event, saving always equals investment (investment is demand or output, less consumption; saving is income less consumption). The saving that people originally wished to do can only be the subject of conjecture. It is through the presence of any of the first four responses listed above that the excess in originally intended saving can be inferred.

The US economy, which has been the central 'user' of excessive Asian savings, initiated responses 1–4 above in that order. First, there was higher investment in the bubble, with a wealth effect that induced lower personal savings. When the bubble burst, the Fed slashed interest rates, reinforcing the fall in personal savings by inducing huge increases in borrowing (more important than lower contractual savings in such vehicles as pension funds and mortgage repayments). The large 2001 tax cut (3) came close behind. When the stockmarket and the economy continued to languish during 2002, the approach was more of the same: another large tax and interest rate cut in 2003 to reinforce the 'Baghdad bounce'. The result has been two years of boom. Policy prescriptions were far more confused in 2001–04 in the euro zone, with correspondingly feeble results until recently.

Why 'invest more' did not work: the bubble, 1998–2000

The story starts with the Asian Crisis of 1997–98. 'Irrational exuberance' was Alan Greenspan's verdict on the US stockmarket before it all started, in December 1996. The Dow Jones Index was at 6,400 and the more representative S&P Index at 740. At the peak of the bubble, three and a half years later in spring–summer 2000, the Dow reached a peak 75% higher at 11,300, and the S&P had more than doubled to 1,520. The Nasdaq 100 Index – the epicentre of tech-bubble folly – had gone up 5.5 times over the same period, from 840 to 4,700. How did Mr Greenspan react to this huge increase in irrationality and exuberance? He encouraged it. Why? At least partly as an indirect response to the 1997 Asian crisis and its aftermath, the massive flow of Asian funds (and repatriated US speculative capital) to the 'safe haven' of the United States. The heavy flow of European capital to the United States began at about the same time, but the state of Europe was not a policy concern to the US authorities.

Increases in interest rates to quell irrational exuberance were put on hold in 1997, partly to avoid reinforcing the already devastating financial consequences of the Asian crisis. In late 1998, in mid-boom for America and Europe, the grossly heightened speculative fever arising from excessive cheap funding (conspicuously in Japanese yen, where a severe recession was coinciding with the Asian crisis) led to the spectacular bankruptcy of Long-Term Capital Management – Russian financial collapse and default being merely its contingent cause. US interest rates were cut three times by Mr Greenspan in seriously misconceived or at best exag-

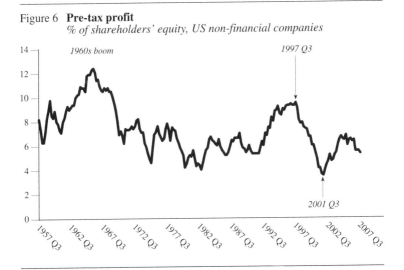

Figure 6 **Pre-tax profit**
% of shareholders' equity, US non-financial companies

gerated anxiety over liquidity. This fuelled the last stage of the stockmarket's stratospheric rise.

The increase in underlying profitability in US business was the true source of the strong 1990s stockmarket. But it was largely over by the middle of the decade: non-financial companies' pre-tax return on net equity nearly doubled from 5.5% in 1990–91 to over 9% by the last quarter of 1994. The stockmarket boom had little to do with high technology, which was just as powerful an innovative factor in the 1980s, when profitability changed little, and the mid-to-late 1990s, when it fell. The drive after 1990 for 'shareholder value' was the root cause of improved profitability, arising (as in Japan after 1997) from 'restructuring'. The search for shareholder value was reinforced by the high cost of borrowing after the turnaround to lower inflation caused by the stringent monetary policy of Paul Volcker, Mr Greenspan's predecessor as chairman of the Fed from 1979 to 1987. Hostile takeovers may not have generated much improvement in overall shareholder value in many instances, as mergers and acquisitions are notoriously unproductive in many, even most cases. But the fear of predators certainly changed behaviour in the managements wishing to survive. (This is the 'Admiral Byng' effect: after the British admiral was shot on a ship's quarterdeck for losing Minorca in 1756, Voltaire remarked that the English 'put an admiral to death now and then, to encourage the others'.)

Once the US corporate return on equity reached 9%, the natural reaction of businesses was 'more of that please'. They wanted more assets on which to earn such returns. Capital spending had been leading the 1990s economic advance since mid-1992, soon after the start of the upswing of profitability; by 1997 the growth rate of real business capital expenditure had been over 10% a year for five years. As the British novelist Kingsley Amis once (in a different context) remarked: 'More means worse.' Economists use the euphemism 'diminishing returns', and it is no coincidence that pre-tax returns to equity, having been on a 9%-plus plateau from late 1994 to 1997, relapsed – just as the capital expenditure growth rate achieved double figures, and stayed there for two and a half years until the bubble burst in mid-2000.

Profitability did not just shrink autonomously, however. The Asian savings excess dates from the Asian crisis, starting in the fourth quarter of 1997 – the same quarter in which the profit downswing began. Asia's economic and financial collapse, with massive devaluations, spurred a frantic search for exports. It was the start of the great surge into surplus. Pricing power weakened in western manufacturing, hitting profits. The concomitant flow of capital to the West underpinned not only booming stock prices, but also the easy debt financing of capital expenditure that helped erode profitability further, through excess capacity. An aspect of the process was upward pressure on the dollar in the late 1990s because of Asian (and European) flows. By putting downward pressure on US manufacturing profits, the high dollar played a part in the substitution of capital inflows for US domestic savings. Industrial capacity utilisation actually fell during the late 1990s, uniquely for a boom period. Just as the stockmarket and economy entered the full flower of leveraged boom, their foundations were being eroded. (The Y2K scare over millennial computer break-downs, a significant influence on Mr Greenspan, added to the spending excess.) The 2–3 year bust starting in mid-2000 was the first example of deflation resulting from balance sheets being trashed by excessive savings inflows from Asia. In this case, Asian surplus flows clearly were not the only factor behind the bubble and bust. But, starting at a crucial phase of the upswing, they reinforced and prolonged it. In an interactive process, excess saving led to lower returns and higher investment via a financial bubble.[3]

The fallacy of 'invest more for the future'

Incidentally, this experience argues against one plausible response to such savings flows: that the West should use the funds to 'invest more' – to 'store up' the benefit of the inflows for the future, for example to take care of future pension funding needs as populations age. It is a fallacy because increasing capital investment in such a fashion depresses returns and profitability; otherwise the savings could not be considered excessive. It can therefore only happen in the private sector in a context in which normal return expectations are distorted by a financial bubble, giving the illusion of strong returns where they are actually falling. Thus, during 1998–2000, financial returns to shareholders looked good, as share prices rose. Yet the return on capital in companies was falling, as excessive investment and the build-up of debt and interest depressed profit margins. It was essentially a liquidity-driven boom, with European and Asian surpluses providing much of the liquidity, reinforced by the Fed. Once share prices had risen to the point where they were liable to 'fall under their own weight', interest rates just happened to have risen enough to constrict liquidity. 'It never rains, but it pours' – and the bubble burst.

The heavy investment in 1998–2000 depended on company managements responding to misconceived shareholder expectations – and in the process undermining them ('more means worse'). It really is not possible for the economy to 'store up future value' with investments that initially yield a poor return. If people knew enough about what the future will require, they would pay for the value with adequate returns right away. In reality, people, including company managements, know very little about precise future needs. The fallacy of knowing the future lies behind much misguided criticism of investor 'short-termism'. If money were spent on the priorities of most 'long-termists', the bankruptcy court would not be far away.

Even where forecasts are right about future needs, the fallacy persists. Suppose you overinvest in correctly chosen productive assets now, to use up excess savings and provide for a future time when population ageing reduces the flow of saving and increasing consumption needs. The overinvestment will create excess capacity, driving down prices. Existing productive assets will be rendered unprofitable, and probably the new assets too. The result is just like a regular bubble: investment stops as it becomes unprofitable, and the economy goes into recession, cutting investment further. Either way, 'investing for the future', a natural financial strategy for individuals, does not work as a real capital spending strategy for society, where the investment is physical, in productive assets, rather than putting money aside.

Only if economies (or societies) lower their expectations of reasonable investment returns can the 'invest more' policy work. But this creates two problems:

- Requiring strong returns is a crucial condition of healthy economic development and should not be abandoned because of the peculiarities of Asian savings behaviour.
- The foreign savings inflows tend to drive up asset prices, at least initially, raising expectations of easy capital gains – the reverse of the lower expectations that are more appropriate.

It is partly because we are still not at the end of this 'bubble' phase of the Asian surplus effects that economies keep going.

The only plausible source for an 'invest more' policy is government investment, especially on infrastructure. This sort of policy, advocated by Keynes in the depression of the 1930s, was adopted by Japan in the 1990s after its late-1980s bubble. Japan's legendary waste and corruption in public projects illustrate the severe limits on such an 'invest more' approach, which is largely self-defeating. Once capital ceases to be perceived as scarce and costly, and starts being thrown around indiscriminately, the hoped-for returns from investment melt away.

Lower private savings: inflation of asset prices – the bubble wealth effect

Private savings rates do not necessarily go down because of lower interest rates. Lower real interest rates (the rate of interest less the rate of inflation) are the true cost of capital, and are driven down by the savings glut. By themselves such lower real rates do not necessarily lower western savings. It is the interaction with prices of real assets – mostly homes and equities – that is crucial to personal savings behaviour.

Before looking at the complexity of personal behaviour, consider the relatively simple case of business savings, which are depreciation plus retained profits (after interest, tax and dividends). Here, the chief driver is profitability itself. In the bubble, business profitability and the spending side of the capital account – investment – were intimately related to one another. After the bubble burst, businesses in both America and Europe reacted to create surpluses: first they cut capital spending, leaving cash flow with which to repay debt; then they raised their cash flow by cutting labour costs. In Japan this had been true since 1997.

If the bubble is accepted as the first phase of the reaction to excessive Asian savings, business behaviour since 2001 can be regarded as exacerbating the surpluses to be absorbed. For Japan and north-central Europe this has already been described. Suffice it to say that in the rest of Europe, and especially the United States, upward shifts in business profitability, and downward pressures on capital spending, have added to the global surplus/savings glut since the bubble burst. Business savings have gone up, in other words, as real interest rates have gone down. This is another example of the importance of getting cause and effect the right way round. It was not that lower interest rates from 2001 would cause lower business saving: it was higher post-bubble business saving that was a major cause of lower interest rates. Reversing the direction of causation reverses the association of savings and real interest rates, as is generally true of cause and effect in economics.

Personal savings can involve a paradox. In an economy with little or no personal holdings of real assets other than owner-occupied homes, low real interest rates might require households to raise savings. Suppose people wish to have a pension pot on reaching 65. If real interest rates are low, the savings rate will need to be higher to accumulate the pot. And low real returns will mean low annuity rates after the age of 65, the pension pay-out period, so that a larger pot will anyhow be required for a desired rate of pension (relative to previous earned income). Thus lower real rates force both a higher proportionate savings rate for a given pot, and a larger pot for a given ratio of pension to previous income. Both these forces generally result in higher savings. Conversely, higher real rates will permit a given ratio of eventual pension to current salary at a lower rate of saving. This idea is uncomfortable for classical economics, as it means that offering a lower rate of return tends to increase savings, and vice versa.

If we introduce personal holdings of equities, a build-up of Asian surpluses flowing into America and the bubble, some things become clearer and others less so. How does the rate of return get lowered by the inflow of surpluses? Why, by rising asset prices: the bubble. For those with assets, the achievement of a desired pension pot is advanced at a stroke by the stockmarket boom. So although the rate of return has been lowered, the all-in return to asset-holders has received a boost. This higher all-in rate of return acts like the higher real rates of the preceding paragraph: by making the pot more easily achieved, it lowers the need to save. This is the wealth effect, leading to a lower savings rate.

This deals with only half the problem, however. The lower real returns resulting from soaring asset prices mean that the annuity/ pension payable from a given pot will be less (especially given increasing longevity). This implies a rising pot – evidence for this being widely publicised and large shortfalls in US and UK company pension plans on proper calculations. It is hard to resist the conclusion that 'Anglo-Saxon' households are adopting an 'ostrich' strategy on this. It looks like a case of inverted Alzheimer's disease. In real Alzheimer's, old people forget the past. With inverted Alzheimer's, middle-aged people forget the future.

Savings needed at 2% and 4% constant real interest rates
Working-life assumptions (with the same real interest rates used for both working-life accumulation of the pension pot, and the resulting annuity paid out from the pot after retirement)

45	year working life (20–65)
20	year retirement (65–85)
3%	annual growth of real income during working life
60%	target pension as % of final salary (fixed for life)
£50,000	final salary

With 2% real interest rates, the required pot is £1,009,456 and the share of salary over the working life required to achieve it is 28.1% (with this share held constant throughout the assumed 45 years of working life).

With 4% real interest rates, the required pot falls by two-thirds to £342,289 and the share of salary is dramatically reduced, to 5.7%.

The strong variation of these figures in relation to what appear to be small changes in real interest rates illustrates the difficulties in the pension debate and for company pension fund provision. Was it Einstein who described compound interest as one of the strongest forces in nature? In reality, pension plans invest heavily (particularly when the members are early in their careers) in higher-risk, higher-return equities, where the long-term real rate of return has been 7%, well above the 2% and 4% considered here. But for this, the pension problems facing most company plans would have been radically worse.

The worst form of inverted Alzheimer's is that the Asian (and European) surpluses are likely on current trends to cause havoc with personal finances through excessive household debt and borrowing. This is the true source of lower savings from lower interest rates. Household savings in aggregate are the net result of saving by savers and net borrowing by households in excess of new home building. With nearly 300 million people in America, for example, there are plenty of households contributing to pension plans and simultaneously paying down mortgages; there are also plenty of households borrowing to buy houses, pay for children's education and so on, so that their consumer spending exceeds their income. If a house-price boom based on capital inflows and fuelled by borrowing drives up consumer spending, the savings rate will be lower, and reasonably closely connected to the low rate of interest. But, of course, the natural ambition – a house with no mortgage and an adequate pension pot at age 65 – is being put on hold by the borrowing. Household debt has to be repaid out of earned income during a working lifetime. Building up debt on the back of higher house prices beyond a certain point is inverted Alzheimer's in this sense: it is in denial of this future requirement. It is this debt behaviour that is the 'bubble' element in western responses to the Asian savings glut in recent years.

But complacency arising from the belief that capital gains will provide the pension pot needed to meet expectations also suggests a major problem arising from lower rates of return on the assets side of personal balance sheets. This mostly concerns America and Britain, where employer-sponsored pensions are important; continental Europeans have much greater reliance on tax-financed public provision with an overlay of private wealth. The resulting equity culture means the wealth effect on saving has been far greater in America and Britain. The continental Europeans have their own peculiar exposure to a huge rise in taxation to fund extravagant public pension promises. But the British and Americans, via public insurance vehicles to make up for private pension scheme failures, may also find themselves with unexpectedly large tax increases on account of widespread failures in private provisions.

Post-bubble monetary and fiscal ease: US policy

US monetary policy was aggressively easy for three and a half years, from early 2001 to mid-2004. Although the bubble peaked in the spring of 2000 – as seen in retrospect, and after numerous revisions of the GDP data for the last three quarters of 2000 – the stockmarket was strong until the end of August. The August average for the S&P index, the representative Wall Street measure, was actually the peak monthly average of the bull market, ahead of springtime monthly averages. In October and as late as December that year well-known US economists were still predicting a soft rather than hard landing for the US economy. (Hard landing is code for virtually no growth, but without necessarily the two quarters of negative GDP that is the technical definition of a recession.) It now turns out that the hard landing was already well under way, for the economy as well as the stockmarket. GDP had fallen as early as the third quarter, recovering a little in the fourth; it was relapsing from just under 5% growth in the year to the second quarter of 2000. Growth was negative again in the first and third quarters of 2001, so that by the second half of 2001 growth from the year before was only just above zero. As sustainable trend growth is (and was) 3% or a little more, the shortfall from this neutral rate was a large three percentage points.

The initial sharp cuts in short-term interest rates were a simple, conventional reaction to the hard landing. The speed and size of the cuts needed was increased by the mistakes made during the bubble. Alan Greenspan carried on talking up the bubble until October 1999, only half a year before it burst – in clear and unjustified contrast to his three years' earlier talk of 'irrational exuberance'. Anti-inflationary interest-rate hikes to keep the economy under control in late 1999 and early 2000 were a classic case of 'too much, too late'. Instead of damping the boom, the Fed aggravated the violence of the cycle and, because Asian inflows had been doing the same, the downswing was correspondingly fierce.

One difference between a bubble and a boom is that after a bubble the distortions introduced in the upswing are so great that it can take two recessions to remove them. (Each boom has its own particular set of distortions that become its Achilles heel. Usually, they involve overextension of the original driving factor that created the boom to start with – in this case business investment.) After the 1999–2000 bubble, it was not so much two recessions as a hard landing and an extremely weak recovery, despite strong policy stimulation (monetary and fiscal). But one implication of the argument in this book is that monetary and fiscal ease have been used to avoid working out the distortions, and that these will soon come back to hit us with another downswing. Recoveries from recession in the United States, where cycles have generally been quite violent, are usually very rapid. But this one was not. After five quarters to the third quarter of 2001 with an average growth rate of just over zero (and three of the five quarters down from the one before), the economy grew at only a feeble 1.75% in the subsequent six quarters. This rate was still well below the 3%-plus trend or potential rate. So from the end of the hard landing as such (in the third quarter of 2001) the shortfall of GDP from its potential level widened substantially further, an extremely unusual and malign development. By early 2003 the economy had been through just under three years at an average growth rate of 1%. By May 2003, fearing deflation, the Fed had cut short-term interest rates to 1%, which was unprecedentedly low and significantly below the inflation rate.

In America and Europe, the end of the bubble resulted in the business sector adding to the potential depression of demand arising from Eurasian surpluses. As the bubble was led by capital expenditure, then burst because of the resulting erosion of profit margins, the reaction in the downswing – and the reason the hard landing started to turn into a deflationary spiral – was to cut capital spending and then raise profitability by cutting jobs and other costs. It is easy to see the deflationary implications of this. But it is useful to view it in terms of flows of funds: each sector's saving minus its investment. In the United States, by spring 2000, business's capital spending exceeded its saving (depreciation plus retained profits) by 2–3% of GDP. By 2003 this had switched to saving (boosted by cost cuts) exceeding capital expenditure by 3–4% of GDP: i.e. this switch shifted the business balance by six percentage points of GDP. The resulting business surplus can be added to the Asian surplus that was financing the capital inflow. With the latter at 5–6% of GDP, the two combined were 9% of GDP. This is a measure of the deficit that had to be run by the combined household and government sectors to keep the economy on an even keel. It is no surprise that such a huge scale of policy stimulation was needed. There has never been anything approaching it in a serious economy in peacetime.

While monetary policy became dramatically easy, arguably the 'heavy lifting' in stimulative policy was done by large tax cuts, an even more extravagant fiscal easing than the monetary stimulus. In January 2001, President George W. Bush came to power committed to tax cuts anyhow. The timing was fortuitous. A large tax cut was proposed and easily passed by Congress in spring 2001. As a result, between 2000 and 2002 the US public-sector balance shifted into deficit by 5.5% of GDP, from more than 1.5% surplus in 2000 to 3.75% deficit in 2002. Of this 5.5% shift, some 4.5% was attributable to policy changes – mostly the tax cut – and the remaining 1% to cyclical losses of tax revenue arising from the recession.

By early 2003, the economy was still languishing with growth below trend. The Iraq war was looming, sapping confidence. With newly elected majorities in both houses of Congress, President Bush implemented another large tax cut, from July 2003. In the second half of 2003, the US public-sector deficit ran at over 5%

of GDP. Tax-cutting policy worsened the balance by 1% of GDP, but some of this was offset by stronger growth giving an autonomous cyclical boost to tax revenue. The combination of large fiscal deficits and the household boom based on easy money – by this time short-term rates had been cut to 1% – coming on top of the post-war 'Baghdad bounce', finally goosed the economy into a boom.

Vibrant economic activity revived tax revenue in 2004 (and 2005), so that the deficit narrowed slightly. Nonetheless, the 2004 US public-sector balance was 6% of GDP worse than in 2000, before the tax cuts. In addition, monetary stimulus had caused the personal-sector deficit to enlarge by 2.5% of GDP. This combined shift of 8.5% of GDP offset the business-sector balance improvement by over 6% plus a 1.5% worsening of the current-account deficit, from 2000's already large 4.25% to 2004's 5.75%. So the business-sector boom–bust partly induced by Eurasian surpluses, together with the increase in the surpluses themselves, was offset by a huge policy-induced boost to US household and government borrowing. Roughly two-thirds of the extra borrowing was being done by government, and one-third by households.

The euro zone's mixed policy response

In the euro zone, such a clear illustration of the shifting flows of funds cannot be made, as it is muddled up with the surplus in Germany and the rest of north-central Europe. The statistics are also vastly inferior. But one of the effects of the monetary union – probably its only major plus-point to date – has been the unification of capital markets, assisting businesses in achieving rapid capital-productivity gains: the same output is being gained from less capital, or more output from the same capital. European business has been throwing off capital. So the euro zone's business financial flows have been improving over the past few years for structural reasons, as well as the post-bubble cyclical restructuring outlined above, in a similar way to the United States.

On the household side, no general economic and monetary union (EMU) pattern can be shown. In Spain, a US/UK-style property boom has proceeded unchecked for years because euro-zone interest rates have been low by Spanish standards. At the opposite end of the spectrum, Germany, growing and inflating the least of the EMU majors, and with the full force of excess savings on both demographic and now restructuring grounds, has seen personal savings grow as housing has declined. Between them come Italy, with German demographics but a poorer housing stock and Spanish reactions to euro interest rates; and France, with stronger demographics but closer to Germany in inflation. For both of these countries, household borrow-and-spend has been a gathering force.

Euro-zone fiscal policy was less fortuitously clear-cut than President Bush's. Apart from the responsibility being at the country level, not 'delegated' (or uplifted) to EMU, any co-ordination that existed was entirely and strongly concerned with eliminating all budget deficits. The background was the major cuts needed in France, Italy and Spain to bring their deficits below 3% of GDP and comply with the Maastricht criteria for EMU membership. Germany, the 'policeman' of EMU, understandably (and rightly) felt that such low deficits in the target year of 1997 might prove a flash in the pan without some continuing restraint of budgetary excesses. The EMU entrants were required to sign up in 1998 to the Stability and Growth Pact (SGP) by which 3% was to be the maximum – allowable only under duress, such as recession – with members committed to budget balance by 2005. This proposal was controversial (to say the least) even before the surplus problem emerged, with Germany in a conspicuous role. One paraphrase of the SGP, for example, was 'Stagnation and Grief Pact'. In the conditions actually prevailing after the bubble burst it was close to a disaster.

The tremendous boom in 1999–2000 actually took the weighted average euro-zone budget balance to a minuscule surplus in 2000 (0.1% of GDP). This was not all that impressive: massive bubble-based tax revenues took America and Britain to 1.5% surpluses in 2000 (excluding one-off UK mobile phone licence proceeds). Still, Italy and Spain got their deficits below 1% of GDP, giving them grounds for patting themselves on the back. However, the onset of recession in 2001 quickly took the gloss off this achievement. The worsening of euro-zone budgets in that year was just under 2% of GDP, only minimally less than the United States with its huge tax cut. At this point policy in the euro zone diverged sharply. Germany, father of the SGP, despite a major private-sector financial surplus that makes it part of the global surplus/deflation problem, decided to add fiscal policy deflation to its (and the world's) woes. Smaller countries (Belgium, Finland, Austria, Ireland and, before strong inflation took its toll, the Netherlands) and Spain emerged comparatively unscathed from the 2001 downswing and sided with Germany. France and Italy took the Anglo-American route and decided not just to accept budget deficits from cyclical tax revenue losses, but to add structural fiscal stimulus on top.

If full employment with low inflation is accepted as the goal of demand management, the euro zone failed utterly (hence the electoral rejection of existing governments in major continental countries recently). But this is not the only criterion for policy, so these fiscal policy responses must be seen in a broader context, bearing in mind that neither exchange-rate nor interest-rate determination is now within the power of national governments. With true political power still firmly in the hands of national governments – and subject to electorates (up to a point) – the confused and transitional nature of the current EMU/government balance of power is inevitable. In a (useful) sense, the severe test it is now being put to will determine more effectively than shallow political decisions in 1996–98 who can genuinely sustain the political integration that is the necessary and painful accompaniment of a true monetary union.

Germany has always been the most ardent advocate of political and economic union as a necessary (ideally pre-) condition of EMU. Suffering an excessive exchange rate on adopting the euro and the highest real interest rates (and bond yields) in the euro zone, as well as the demographic and restructuring deflation, it might be thought perverse to the point of masochism for Germany to have added fiscal tightness as a fifth source of demand restraint. But at least at the level of the ruling elite it had two other priorities: first, to make the monetary union, in which its ruling class has always been the most fervent and serious believer, a success; and second, to shed the excessive labour costs built up in 1990–97 as a result of German reunification. Quintuple German deflation (exchange-rate, monetary, fiscal, demographic and restructuring) may have caused three recessions in three years, but it has imposed labour-market flexibility – by brute force. As a result, Germany is now able to gain market share both within the euro zone and outside it, and probably over time to enjoy faster productivity growth, raising long-term income growth. Other countries' fiscal policies have reflected their own particular circumstances. These will be clearer after a look at how monetary policy was managed in the post-bubble stagnation.

The nature of the monetary union, still in its early days, ensured monetary policy was also confused, especially in appearance. Appearances and 'credibility' (market trust) are important for effective monetary policy: the US Fed's presentation of its policy has been assured, and its reputation is high, even if that policy can be quite severely criticised in its substance. Much public confusion about the policies of the European Central Bank (ECB) arises from the importance of Germany, which accounts for 30% of EMU GDP (the combination of deflationary factors in Germany, many related to the euro, is described above). But the ECB has to consider the whole of the euro zone, 70% of which is not Germany. With German inflation mostly in the 1–2% range, and growth minimal, why not ease monetary policy? The answer is because conditions are very different elsewhere. In Germany, the real three-month interbank interest rate has been 2% and

Figure 7 **3-month euro-Libor**
'Real' cost adjusted for inflation in selected countries, %

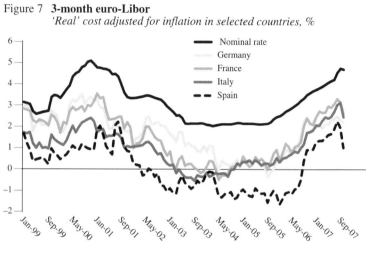

falling since post-bubble 2001 and has become steadily less burdensome. But the real rate for France, Italy and especially Spain has been zero to negative for over two and a half years. For EMU as a whole, real short-term rates have been as low as in the United States. While its long-term trend growth has been weaker, the level of GDP vis-à-vis this trend has been less depressed than America's at the worst, and the inflation rate has stayed up stubbornly. This is why ECB policy could be regarded as in aggregate easier, or at least no tighter, than the Fed's.

The true source of slow euro-zone growth, apart from Germany's multiple deflation, is the dismal long-term trend (or 'potential') growth rate. This is caused by supply-side weaknesses such as excessive and distorted taxation, overregulation and, most conspicuously, labour-market rigidities that make it difficult and costly to fire people and place restrictions on working hours. These problems are not the subject here. Combined with now-static, EMU-wide, working-age-group growth, the effect of these productivity constraints on long-term growth trends is to cut it below 2% for the euro zone, more than 1% annually behind the US and 0.5% behind Britain. The effect of this feeble trend, alongside restrictive policies that have actually managed to get EMU GDP below it – if by less than the US at the worst of its hard landing (first quarter of 2003) – has been lethal to the global economic standing of the euro zone. Such is the price of the ill-considered rush to 'union'. But the positive result is that whatever (almost certainly reduced) monetary union emerges from current conditions will be a serious entity, unlike what was put together in 1991–99.

With monetary policy outside the control of euro-zone countries, it is only against this backdrop that we can see their fiscal policies in a proper perspective. France, which was close to average in terms of inflation rate and therefore real interest rates, pursued moderate budget stimulation after 2001, with no serious regard for the SGP. This has been largely successful: France's demand management policies have been closest to those of America and Britain. Its house-price boom has been strong. The economy has deviated relatively little from long-term trend growth rates. Its high unemployment, like its slow trend growth, are functions of labour-market and other supply-side policies, which include making it illegal to work hard – the 35-hour week – and are utterly unlike America's and Britain's. But from the standpoint of accommodating Eurasian surpluses, French policy has been increasingly successful.

The same is not true of Spain and Italy, which are also very different from one another. In Spain, the starting point was productivity at some 85% of the level in Germany, France and Italy (all of which were very close in real output per worker-hour in 1999); but having much lower labour costs, only about half Germany's. The natural effect of the fixed exchange-rate regime was to ensure both faster growth than the rest of EMU – real income catch-up – and faster inflation, thereby achieving cost convergence. (Low inflation and currency appreciation was the alternative route chosen by Japan and Germany in the 1970s and 1980s.)

Faster Spanish inflation meant that the common interest rates and bond yields for the euro were much lower in real terms than for Germany and France. Though Spain's growth has not been impressive given its potential – and productivity trends have worsened – it is not for lack of demand. The house-price and real estate boom has equalled or surpassed that of America, Britain and France, fuelled by ultra-cheap money and price levels that were low to start with. Fiscal policy has been quite rightly concerned with stemming some of these speculative excesses, and the structural budget balance has tightened. Spain is thus able to look down on fellow euro-zone countries, neither breaching the SGP with budgetary ease, as France and Italy have done, nor resorting, as Germany has, to simple, recession-induced tax shortfalls. It is a feel-good mix to match America's in response to the inflow of the Asian savings glut.

Italy's policy has been seemingly like France's, but with key flaws. While its labour costs have grown only 0.5% a year faster than France's, its productivity growth has been negligible for the full seven years' existence of the euro. This is euro-sclerosis at its most extreme. A widening budget deficit has been needed as much to compensate with artificial stimulus for loss of export competitiveness vis-à-vis EMU 'partners' as to offset Eurasian surpluses. In the current global boom, with borrowing costs for Italians unprecedentedly low, mortgage finance growing at nearly 20% a year is adding to budget action to keep the economy on the move as Italy, the Cinderella of EMU, keeps seeing its market share poached by the ugly sisters to the north. But its unit labour costs have gone adrift by 15% compared with the rest of the euro zone since 1998, and the gap is widening by 2% a year (more compared with Germany, of course). Unlike Spain, Italy's labour costs when EMU started in 1999 were above Germany's, similar to France and Benelux. Eurasian surpluses are in effect papering over a crack that has become so wide that Italy will probably have to give up EMU membership (painfully) in a few years. The ready availability of Eurasian surpluses while problems are quietly swept under the carpet may do neither Italy nor its euro-zone partners any favours.

Britain's fortunate policy framework

In Britain, where the growth trend has not deteriorated, the shift of responsibility for setting interest rates from the government to the Bank of England (BoE) in May 1997 has been fortuitously helpful to handling the Asian savings excess, aside from its intrinsic merits. The government simply sets the BoE an inflation target and leaves it to set interest rates to achieve that target. This separation of the goal (or end) of monetary policy – constant inflation at 2% (now, for the consumer price index; 2.5% initially in 1997 for a modified version of the retail price index) – from the means (interest rates) has been highly beneficial in ways that go well beyond the simple removal of political temptations to meddle with rates. The single-tasked BoE has to be forward-looking, in a way the US Fed certainly is not. Setting rates with respect to a forecast of inflation two years hence (or whatever period is suitable) forces discipline on both the forecasting process and the discussion of appropriate rates. This can otherwise be only too easily influenced by short-term fluctuations in economic and financial market conditions and/or confidence, as has been normal in America.

Moreover, by imposing the inflation target as the framework for monetary policy, the BoE's independence removes the need and temptation for central bankers to involve and compromise themselves politically. It is common to hear central bankers express views on such matters as the budget deficit, rigidities in the labour market and so forth (all of them the subject of speeches by Fed and ECB members in recent years). Now the BoE simply has to say, for example about an increase in the government deficit, that achievement of the inflation target will require higher interest rates the larger the government deficit is. Whether the central bankers approve or disapprove of the fiscal policy – which is politically irrelevant and arguably unconstitutional – becomes irrelevant to their monetary role. Note the contrast with the ECB, which not only sets its own targets – in this case for broad money growth as well as inflation – but also is independent by international treaty (Maastricht) rather than by (revocable) legislative action. The ECB has significantly raised perceptions that its policy is unduly tight by combining interest rate decisions with scolding various member states for policy errors, which in a democracy is not within its remit. Mr Greenspan has been only marginally less gratuitous.

The BoE remit was well suited to handling the Asian savings glut and the bubble and bust of 1999–2002. The BoE was lucky in that at the start of the new regime in mid-1997, inflation was about on the set target, growth was about on trend, and so was the level of GDP. The remit came down to keeping growth on trend (2.5% on most independent estimates) and to avoiding any build-up of inflationary pressures from overheating or disinflationary pressures from inadequate demand. As above-trend growth pressure mounted in the bubble, inflation forecasts tended to rise, so it was felt that interest rates were increased in plenty of time. But this timely shift of monetary policy towards higher interest rates, combined with the Asian surplus sloshing about looking for a well-run safe haven, meant that sterling rose. In Britain's very open economy, this created immediate downward pressure on prices – the target of monetary policy – as well as on export demand and manufacturing profitability. As a result, easing of demand pressure reinforced cheaper imports to cut inflation.

While freedom of the flow of capital into and out of Britain has never been threatened, such flows have also (fortuitously) been less problematic than for the United States in recent years.

Britain has an 'unencumbered' currency. The US dollar, however, has reserve currency status. It is an uncomfortable position, as funds move into and out of the dollar for reasons unconnected to the US economy, but it is also profitable. The US financial industry benefits hugely from such flows. But this position has been massively complicated in recent years by China's pegging its currency to the dollar, together with its emergence as a major trading power. Britain has been able to get the best of both worlds on this point: it is a major beneficiary of global financial flows, but without compromise to its monetary independence.

3

International monetary consequences: the New Dollar Area

China pegged the yuan to the dollar in 1994 in good faith as a stabilising measure after the major 1994 devaluation. This followed loss of monetary control and 30% inflation in 1993. Ironically, the yuan–dollar peg has been a major destabilising force in recent years. In effect, it prevented the adjustment of exchange rates that would otherwise have occurred from early 2002. The dollar, unlike sterling, cannot float freely if other countries insist on pegging their currencies to it, in its role as the world's reserve currency. After private-capital flows into the dollar dried up in early 2002, it should have been possible for it to depreciate to the level at which investors recovered their appetite, probably with higher bond yields as part of the bargain. This might or might not have involved improvement in the US current deficit, or perhaps the lessening of some of the Eurasian surpluses. But it would have balanced out the financing of such imbalances with the cost-benefit analysis of investors providing the counterpart capital flows. The drastic cuts in US short-term

Figure 8 **Weighted average exchange rates adjusted for relative unit labour costs**
Except China based on relative consumer prices, April 2001 = 100

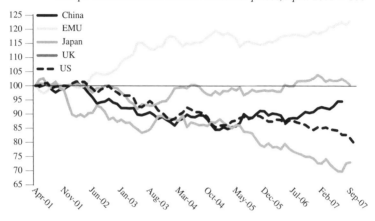

Sources: IMF; Federal Reserve broad index (US)

interest rates in 2001–03 were at least partly intended to achieve this prophylactic decline in the dollar. Because of the yuan–dollar peg, it did not happen.

Between the yuan–dollar peg's establishment in 1994 and now, China has made a quantum leap in global economic significance. It is the dominant economy regionally, given its greater participation in foreign trade than Japan. The yuan–dollar peg gave support to the Pacific region during the gross upheavals of the 1997–98 Asian crisis. But the increased size of China, and its huge advantage in cost competitiveness, has been an increasing concern for Asian countries from Japan downwards. Over the past 15–20 years they have been 'hollowed out' by China's takeover of much of the world's manufacturing. The combination of the yuan–dollar peg and the dollar's decline from early 2002 confronted Asian competitors with the risk of even greater Chinese cost competitiveness. Their response was what we call the New Dollar Area (NDA), a semi-fixed-rate currency zone including China, Japan and the Asian Tigers, bound together by the mortar of fear – fear of China. Japan and those Asian Tigers without existing dollar pegs managed their exchange rates by intervention to ensure they stayed competitive – not with the dollar, as US competition is not a problem, but with China and its yuan.

As a result, the 12–15% cut in America's real exchange rate over three years from early 2002 – i.e. the gain in its global cost competitiveness with trading partners – was roughly matched by the real trade-weighted yuan exchange rate and China's cost advantage – and, surprise, surprise, by Japan's, together with that of much of the rest of the Asian Tigers. In effect, the dollar was able to devalue only against the euro and sterling. Almost all the Eurasian structural surpluses corresponding to the US deficit lie in Pacific Asia (Japan, China and the Tigers), with which America made no gain in cost competitiveness. Those countries had their costs heavily trimmed vis-à-vis Europe's, and the European market-share gains that resulted were achieved much more by Asian rather than American exporters. And in the US market itself, Asians were able to gain share from Europeans faster than had been occurring in any case. With Asian/US competitiveness locked in place by the NDA structure, America's US expansion raised its imports and ensured no deficit reduction was achieved by the dollar devaluation. On the contrary, between 2000 and

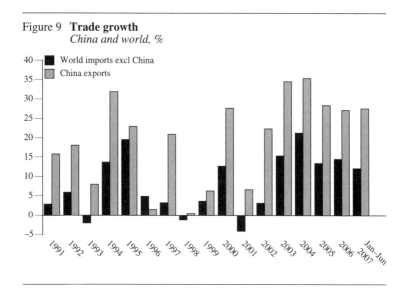

Figure 9 **Trade growth**
China and world, %

2005 the US current-account deficit rose from 4% of GDP to
6–6.5%. Some adjustment!

That China had no need of extra cost-competitive advantage
can be seen by examining its export growth vis-à-vis world trade
(see Figure 9). In 2002, as the recovery from the bubble started,
world imports excluding China grew by 3%; China's exports grew
a strong 22%. Yet pre-yuan depreciation relative costs at the end
of 2001 will have underlain this performance. China certainly did
not need an extra 12% of cost competitiveness. It hung onto the
dollar partly through inertia and partly through an understandable
desire for stability, given the upheavals of 1993–94 and its relative
strength in (and immunity from) the Asian crisis of 1997–98, in
which the rigidity of the dollar peg was a help.

But increasingly China's policy looks like crude, muscle-bound mercantilism: a simple, zero-sum-game attempt to grab export market share by exchange-rate manipulation. Though the rest of the Asian NDA countries tag along behind willingly enough, Chinese policymakers must take a major share of responsibility for the more extreme destabilising effects of Asian surpluses which are the subject of this book. But before looking at the global consequences, the effects of China's policy on its own development, and on its savings and surplus, must be understood. It is a classic case of how mercantilism tends over time to damage the apparent market-share winner, via a variety of feedbacks.

In 2002–04, China's depreciation seemed superficially innocuous, because its current-account surplus (unlike that of Japan and the Asian Tigers) barely increased. It was possible to claim that the yuan–dollar peg was not causing Chinese under-valuation. But the underlying dynamics were not simply a matter of short-term shifts in the trade balance, and the gross under-valuation is now being revealed by the exploding surplus that emerged in 2005. The key is the domestic Chinese boom induced by the downswing of the yuan. To hold its rate against the dollar, China and other Asian NDA countries managing their exchange rates had to intervene heavily to buy dollars and sell their own currencies. This led to vast flows of liquidity being flushed out into their domestic financial systems as well as huge accumulations of dollar reserves, with important consequences in 2005 (see page 206).

Soaring domestic liquidity created a credit-financed investment boom in China; in Japan it underpinned the end of the long spiral of deflation (see page 190). China's boom sucked in a huge flow of imports, keeping its Chinese surplus down. Most of these imports, apart from energy and raw materials, were from Japan and the Tigers. If we regard the Asian end of the NDA – China, Japan and the Tigers (the entire Pacific Rim) – as a semi-fixed-rate block, the undervaluation of their currencies as a group is demonstrated by their rapidly growing collective surplus: the distribution of that surplus was simply loaded away from China and into the others by the Chinese investment boom temporarily sucking in imports from Japan and the Tigers. As this Chinese domestic boom unwinds, the primary role of yuan undervaluation emerges.

China's official figures for real GDP growth cannot be believed. Growth for the past ten years is said to have varied between 7% and 10%, an incredibly narrow range given the importance of invest-ment, which is invariably a more volatile part of demand than consumption – it is not far short of half GDP. The nominal data (i.e. the original numbers before adjustment for price changes) can be adjusted by separately published inflation figures to give a rough idea of real growth; this shows an altogether more plausible cyclicality. In 1998–99, affected by the Asian crisis, nominal growth was only 5% in each year. For six quarters running it averaged about 4%; allowing for slight deflation at the time, implied real growth was only 4–5%. By contrast, in 2004 nominal growth was 16.5%. Domestic inflation was about 3%, with much of the 4% consumer price index gain reflecting the higher costs of imported oil, food and raw materials, so real GDP growth was 13–14%. In other words, China's trend growth is about 8–9%, as claimed, but with a much more plausibly violent cyclical range of

Figure 10 **China: GDP and trade and domestic demand**
Nominal data, % change over 4 quarters

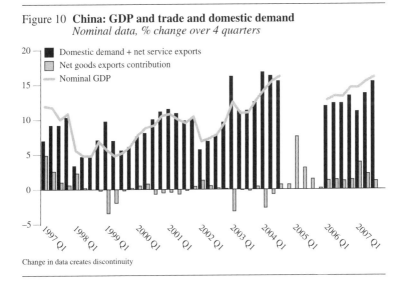

Change in data creates discontinuity

plus or minus 4–5% (i.e. from 4% to 13%) rather than the plus or minus 1.5% implicit in the published real growth figures.

The importance of this lies in the domestic boom it reveals in 2003–04, when nominal domestic demand was up by 16–18% on the year earlier level for three quarters at the peak. Net exports made a slightly negative contribution because the surge of imports was temporarily even greater than the surge of exports. As the domestic boom has inevitably ebbed away, the surge of exports has continued. Import growth has fallen back, in line with domestic demand – though imports of parts for assembly and export have continued to grow fast. Year-on-year domestic demand growth for the first three quarters of 2005 averaged about 8% nominally (perhaps 6% in real terms). Import growth fell from 38% in 2004 to 16% in 2005. Net exports have contributed nearly half the growth of nominal GDP and more than that in real terms, given little if any inflation of export prices and continually rising costs of imported oil and raw materials. But for export growth, the fall-back of domestic demand would probably have led to an immediate hard landing in response to the excessive capital spending of 2003–04. Export growth has provided jobs and wages in export industries that have softened (so far) the drop in domestic demand growth.

Several consequences of the yuan–dollar peg for the global economy worsened financial imbalances in 2003–04:

- Excessive export competitiveness in Asia, which much increased its surplus.
- Fear of deflation in 2002 and early 2003 as the United States was unable to raise demand by rebalancing overseas accounts with exports. This provoked extreme monetary and fiscal measures in spring 2003 that sowed the seeds of a debt crisis. There is also a continuing need to manage demand that runs at 106–107% of income and output: an almost impossible task.
- Huge deflation of euro-zone demand as it bore the brunt of exchange-rate adjustment against both the dollar and Asia at a time when the introduction of the euro and confused allocation of policy formation – indeed a complete absence of it in the case of foreign exchange-rate policy. This meant that demand collapsed even more severely for three years than it need have, despite already inadequate policies.
- China lurched away from market-oriented development after a boom–bust that will leave it painfully exposed if (as is likely) a US

downswing hits it just when it seeks good growth ahead of the 2008 Olympics.

On the plus side must be mentioned at least two benefits, the second probably temporary and likely to be painfully reversed:

- Japan was helped in finally checking its apparently unstoppable downward deflationary spiral.
- America's appetite for consumption and house-price gains was satisfied by easy money. This was a substitute for sustaining growth with continued rebalancing of its international accounts via some export growth. Asian economies were happy to provide the US with credit – 'vendor financing' in effect – achieving development at the expense of, for the time being, effectively giving away the resulting product.

4

House prices and household dis-saving: the debt build-up

Simple borrowing growth has cut household savings rates throughout most of the developed world, starting with America, Britain and Australia, and followed by parts of continental Europe, especially Spain and France. In Japan the personal savings rate has also decreased, but not through borrowing: the chief cause has been a generation passing through the age of 65 and changing from high, late-career savers to low-saving pensioners. The rise of household borrowing has generally been in parallel with rapid growth of house prices. The huge flow of funds from the Asian surpluses has provided a liquidity base from which banks have been able to expand their business by lending against homes. This surge of buying power has driven up the price of these homes and raised borrowing power, in a virtuous circle. Easy monetary policies have been the immediate driver of this process. Much of the borrowing has been to finance consumption, hence the lower savings rates. Increased new housing investment has also been a significant feature.

The increase in house prices has chiefly reflected two factors:

Figure 11 **House prices**
1996 = 100

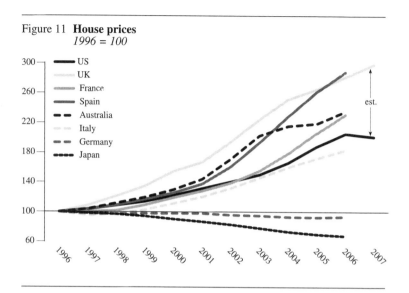

easy monetary policy to accommodate the Asian surpluses with current-account and domestic household deficits, as already outlined, and demographics. Thus Britain, with relatively easy monetary policies over the past seven or eight years and a strong flow of immigration to boost the labour force, has, along with Australia and Spain, had the largest house-price gains. Spanish prices have been boosted by easy money: the common euro interest rates (both short- and long-term) have been lower than Spanish inflation and therefore highly stimulative. France and the United States have lagged behind these three. In France, monetary policy and population trends probably boost house prices less than in America, but French house prices were notoriously low to start with. Italy, like Germany, suffers from a falling working-age population, but euro interest rates are far more stimulative in Italy (almost as much as in Spain) than in Germany. The result has been quite lively Italian house-price growth. In Japan all asset prices, including real estate, have been in a downward spiral from grossly excessive levels in its bubble (see below). Japan also suffered from the onset of a falling working-age population in the 1990s, before Germany and Italy.

House-price inflation took off after 2001, when interest rates were slashed in response to the recession. The phrase 'echo-bubble' gets its force from this handing over of the asset-price baton from the stockmarket in 1998–2000 to the housing market. While the idea of serial bubbles is an appealing metaphor for asset-price booms 'inflated' by the restless Asian surplus, the word bubble for an asset-price boom implies the expectation of a drastic fall when the 'bubble' is 'burst'. That seems unlikely to happen to house prices in the near future. House-price gains will be shown to be a much more logical and sustainable response to the Asian surpluses than stockmarket gains. But this has to be seen in a broad-brush global context as it has developed over the past 17 years.

In 1988, the developed world economy had settled down after the oil crises and a variety of early-1980s upheavals. But (as described at the start of this book) bolting onto the world economy the countries of the former Soviet Union, 1.25 billion Chinese and 1 billion Indians meant productive assets were suddenly in short supply relative to labour and potential labour. Prices of all assets therefore went up, but most of all those of productive assets. Hence the asset-price bubble initially (in the

1990s) was concentrated in the stockmarket (outside Japan). The huge extra supply of labour reinforced monetary stringency in cutting down inflation. So bond prices also gained mightily. But growth in China and India, though rapid, is less impressive relative to their low level of incomes – i.e. large catch-up potential – and rates of capital investment. This is by comparison with European growth in the 1950s and 1960s, and Japan and South Korea in the 1960s and 1970s.[4] The savings glut is associated with and partly the result of this inadequate growth performance. A global shortage of productive assets, resulting in their prices rising, should have provoked faster development of Asian emerging economies. This should have involved higher consumer spending, given their poverty, as well as investment. It has not, and excessive savings are one result. So the boom in asset prices has switched naturally from productive assets (the stockmarket) to land (property or real estate) as these surpluses seek a home, aided by the gearing of cheaper debt.

In principle, lower interest rates favour most the prices of the longest-lasting assets, which ultimately means land. This argument can be developed either by examining property, real estate and land as investment assets, or by considering the position of a person intending to finance a purchase of a house with borrowed money. In either case, a fundamental point is that variations in the price of land are the chief element in variations of the price of real estate in general, or houses in particular. It is common to observe that the same house will have different values in, for example, London and rural Scotland: hence the property person's constant refrain 'location, location, location'.

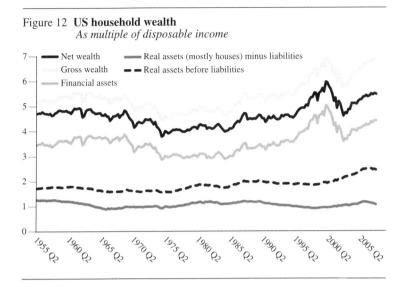

Figure 12 **US household wealth**
As multiple of disposable income

Likewise, variations over time in the cost of a house in a given place are generally only weakly connected to replacement, or building, costs. The remainder of such variation over time reflects movements in the value of the land (or location).

Viewed in terms of return on an investment asset, the rent on real estate is 'real' – i.e. inflation-protected – on the normal assumption that land at least holds its value in the long run. The real rate of interest, if falling, therefore provides a justification for lower rental rates. But if rental yields fall from 6% to 5%, for example, without any change in the actual cash rent being paid, the value of the real estate will increase by 6/5, or 20%. For example, imagine a property yielding £6,000 in rent. If rental yields are 6%, its value is £100,000. If rental yields fall to 5%, its value will go up to £120,000, as the £6,000 rent is 5% of

£120,000. £120,000 is of course 20% up from £100,000, a ratio of 6/5, the inverted change in rental rate.

In 1985–2000, the yield of long-term bonds decreased a lot because of lower inflation, but the real yield (nominal, or actual, yield minus inflation) stayed high, typically around 4–5% for US government debt. Two leveraged booms, end-1980s and end-1990s, saw to that. Also, the bond-market scars from high inflation ensured that investors brought yields down 'behind' inflation, so that the yield differential above inflation, i.e. the real yield, remained high. High real yields meant real estate and housing did not do particularly well. But from 2001, real yields fell as stockmarkets crumbled and business worldwide shifted its finances from net borrowing to net lending. These conditions are highly favourable to real estate in general, specifically land prices, including housing.

Affordability

Perhaps an easier way to see why much higher house prices are justified is to look at the 'affordability' of borrowing to buy a house, i.e. the ability of people to afford the cost of a typical mortgage. Affordability reflects three phenomena: the income available to support a mortgage; the house price needing to be financed; and the interest rate and term of the mortgage. In effect, lower inflation and interest rates make long-lasting assets like houses more affordable, because they make genuinely long-term loans possible. For example, a £100,000 25-year loan at a 12%

rate of interest when inflation is 8% will lead to a payment of about £12,750 a year. Of the £12,750 in the first year, £8,000 is the inflation element in the interest rate, £4,000 is the 'real' interest element and £750 is the principal repayment. But while the lender is owed £99,250 in theory at the end of year one, in real terms (allowing for inflation) the value of the amount outstanding is 8% less than this. In effect, the £8,000 inflation element in the first year's payment was capital repayment: compensation to the lender for the effect of inflation on the principal value of the loan. But this large, immediate, inflation-adjusted reduction of the principal outstanding is a heavy burden for the borrower.

Take away excessive inflation, and affordability of loans improves. A loan bearing a 6% rate with inflation at 2% has the same 4% real interest rate. But the annual payment is only £7,820, nearly £5,000 less than in the 12% case. The capital repayment in year one is £3,820, inflation-adjusted for only 2% in this case, rather than £8,750 in the 12% loan example. The lower inflation and interest rate makes the repayment much less burdensome. If lower real interest rates are layered onto this, the position becomes even more favourable. With the same 2% inflation rate, a real interest rate of 2% (half the 4% real rate used so far) would mean a total interest rate payable of 4%. The £100,000 loan over 25 years then comes down in annual cost to £6,400. It is not hard to see why lower inflation followed by lower real interest rates has led to higher house prices. People can simply afford more.

In America, the National Association of Realtors computes its own affordability index, which is based on 100 when a family on the median income can just afford a mortgage on the going

Figure 13 **US and UK housing affordability indices**

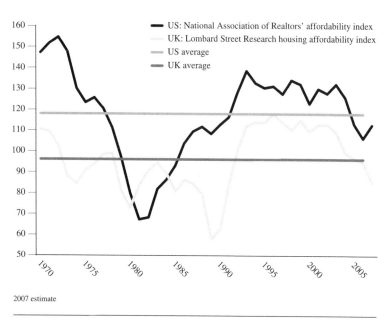

2007 estimate

terms on a house at the median price. The going terms were much improved by lower interest rates in the period since the index started in 1981. The mortgage rate hit its high at over 16% in 1981–82, settled down at just over 10% in 1986–90, and then came down steadily through the 1990s to 7–8% in 1999–2000, and under 6% in 2003–04. Only recently has the acceleration of house-price inflation to the mid-teens brought affordability down to the level of 1990, and it remains above that of the 1980s.

In Britain, affordability is probably better at this point than in the United States. Looking at the mortgage cost (over 25 years) of the average house price for the average household income at the going rate of interest, or simply relating house prices and/or mortgage amounts taken out to the average incomes declared on application forms, the 2004 level of affordability is the same or slightly better than in 1984–87, and far better than in the bubble years of 1989–90. This appears to contradict the all-time record ratio of house prices to average earnings. But that ratio takes account neither of the reductions in mortgage interest rates (which helps affordability) nor of the increased number of incomes supporting the average mortgage. The increase in two-income mortgages means that today's average mortgage is supported by 1.6 incomes compared with 1.2 incomes 15 years ago. This raises house-price affordability relative to average earnings. Despite the large gains in UK house prices, affordability appears to compare quite favourably with the past.

Dangers of the debt burden

The danger in the debt-financed run-up of house prices lies not so much in the price levels so far achieved as in the debt burden taken on. Moreover, the new debt that has to be taken up each year for households to 'do their bit' in using up the Eurasian surplus may require that acceptable affordability now will not last, as house prices have to carry on up to keep households borrowing. This immediately removes continental Europe from the risk list. Whereas household liabilities relative to disposable income have shot up to 160% in Britain and 125% in the US, in continental

Europe only in Germany are they over 100%. Germany has no house-price inflation and very low short- and long-term interest rates: it is out of the 'borrow-and-spend' game, which is part of the savings-glut problem, not the 'spend today, worry tomorrow' solution. In France, Italy and Spain household liabilities are in the region of 60% of disposable income. The reasons for this vary by country, but common features are very light use of housing debt to finance consumption, and, until recently, relatively primitive financial systems ill-adjusted to the needs of households rather than business (rather like the Asian developing countries although somewhat further on than them). Continental European housing debt is largely for house purchase, and is generally a smaller proportion of the house price with more arduous conditions. By contrast, the Anglo-Saxon world has used its housing collateral for equity withdrawal by means of refinancing mortgages at a higher level, as rates have come down, or by borrowing under second-mortgage facilities.

Vulnerability arising from high debt can take at least two forms, leaving aside loss of work or being obliged to take a lower-paying job. First, the relatively benign affordability analysis above is correct only in terms of the cash-flow financing capacity of households confronted with higher house prices. It does not alter the fact that new debt burdens are real, and last longer in a non-inflationary environment. In the 1980s, new home-buyers might have been stretched to afford their monthly mortgage payments, but they could reflect that a few years of wage or salary increases at inflated rates would make those payments far less of a burden. In other words, the high initial effective repayment in inflationary

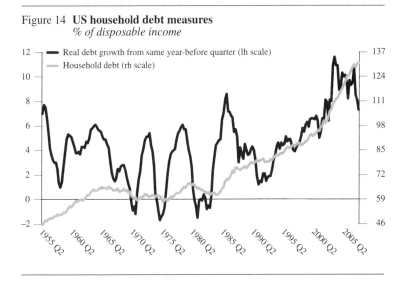

Figure 14 **US household debt measures**
% of disposable income

conditions had its corollary in later relief. This is a slow-burn drawback to taking on a 'full-stretch' mortgage in present conditions, but a real enough one. More immediately serious, of course, is that a high debt burden relative to income means that households are affected much more by increases in interest rates. And the impact of a 0.5% rise in rates will be proportionately much larger at low interest rates than high ones, even before allowing for the newly high debt ratio to income. In America, rising interest rates are an everyday reality.

Moreover, sustaining world demand, and preventing a depression resulting from the Asian savings excess, requires western households to continue each year to add debt and raise their debt/income ratio. US households have increased their real debt outstanding by just under 10% of disposable income for the past 2–3 years. (In nominal terms, the annual debt increase has been 12–13% of disposable income.) But the trend rate of US GDP growth, and therefore real income, is at or just above 3%. (Real income has grown faster recently because of tax cuts and the resulting boom, but further tax cuts to sustain such growth are not in prospect, given the scale of the budget deficit.) With household liabilities now 125% of disposable income, of which debt is nearly 120 percentage points, the increase of real debt is 8–9% of existing liabilities. Growth of liabilities at 8–9%, where real income is growing at only 3%, really is unsustainable. Yet that is what is required to keep the world economy on an even keel. Clearly, such growth in liabilities is only possible even in the short term as long as house prices boom – and boom they must until they are beyond affordability.

Before working out this iron logic – the anvil on which the world economy is likely to be broken – it is necessary to connect the western economic experience to that of China and the Tigers. Also, an understanding of the forces at work is enormously helped by looking at the Japanese experience, which since its bubble in 1989 has been a 'dry run' for many of the issues and problems addressed here.

5

Excess savings and Japan, 1989–2005: debt and pension shortfalls compounded

Japan's late-1980s bubble was followed by its 'long night of the '90s'. This gives some useful hints about the forces at work – it is no coincidence that Japan has been a major part of the current Eurasian surplus problem. There are major differences between Japan's particular experience and the global story in recent years. But there are also major points in common: lessons that can be learned by policymakers, if they so wish, and by anyone who wants to understand what is going on and what the future may hold. A crucial common point is that a structural excess of savings has been a large part of Japan's problems for the better part of 20 years.

Until the mid-1980s, Japan had a high personal (household) saving rate, but a conventional rate of business saving (i.e. depreciation plus retained profit). In the United States, for example, business savings have for the past 25 years been in the region of 12–13% of GDP. Japan's was just above this, but for a country with a trend growth rate of 5%, i.e. still in catch-up mode rather

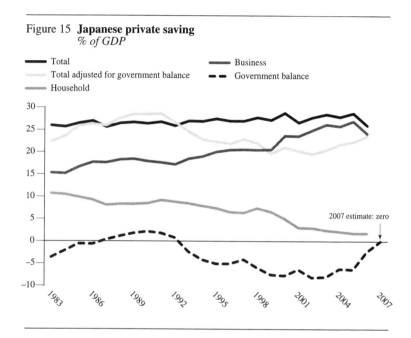

Figure 15 **Japanese private saving**
            % of GDP

than a mature economy, it was not out of line. As the late 1980s
bubble developed, this pushed upwards to around 17–18%.
Household saving remained high. The boom boosted government
tax receipts and its accounts went into surplus. The combination
of private saving and government balance moved to 28% of GDP,
an increase of 5–6 percentage points over 5–6 years.

This was excessive saving at the national level. Because the
bubble involved – in fact was led by – strong business investment, industrial capacity soared. Excess capacity held down
inflation. Monetary policy, with the Bank of Japan (BoJ) seeing
little inflation, was not particularly tight. So the current-account
surplus was not particularly large: the savings were being used

in the home market for overinvestment. This provided a fairly clean analogy with the 1998–2000 US bubble, which was the first-round effect of excessive Asian savings after the Asian crisis ten years later.

As well as the similarities in the generation of the two bubbles – each reflecting huge liquidity expressing itself in asset prices and overinvestment rather than consumer price inflation – there was further similarity in the leveraging up of business with debt. But Japan's bubble was a lot more noxious than the 1998–2000 bubble for a number of reasons:

- As well as a stockmarket bubble, real estate prices reached ridiculous heights, to the extent that the Emperor's Palace was assessed to be worth more than California. In the long 1990–2003 bear market, real estate as well as stock prices fell by 80% or so.
- Japan's demographic trend was changing. From labour force growth in the 1980s, it slowed to stagnation and then a falling working-age population in the 1990s. This tended to increase (late-career) saving and simultaneously decrease capital spending needs, especially on construction. The excess saving, i.e. demand deficiency, was aggravated. This has been an early-2000s problem in Europe, but less so in America.
- The end of the 1980s marked the end of Japan's fast-growth catchup development. The growth trend in the 1980s was just under 5%, well ahead of the United States and western Europe. In the 1990s, partly through the effects of the working-age population reversal, the long-run trend GDP growth rate fell dramatically to about 1%. This too is mirrored in the post-2000 euro zone, lower

growth trends being associated, as in Japan, with the demographic downswing.

- The sharp fall in trend growth meant the old habit of loading firms with debt would not be justified by 'growing out of trouble'. And debt ratios in Japan in 1990 were in any case higher than in the United States ten years later.
- US policy took a year or two to react fully to the bubble bursting. Firms were restructuring hard by the end of 2001. But Japan was in denial from 1990 until 1996, during which time debt ratios and excess capacity got much worse.
- Japan's top-down, directed development system had worked quite well in securing catch-up growth, but proved a serious liability once economic maturity was achieved. The shift to a bottom-up, market-based system with firms aiming for shareholder value has been a big wrench. Again, the analogy is with core euro-zone countries since 2000, but not America.

Clearly, the US bubble was less serious than the one ten years previously in Japan, and the immediacy of action limited the damage. For example, between 1990 and 1997, when Japan finally took on the full challenge of its bubble, government debt rose from 60% to 100% of GDP, and the lurch into deficit had become chronic dependency. The reason for Japan's delay was that its bubble posed a far deeper challenge to Japanese society, politics and policymaking than the US bubble did. (We shall see later how elements of denial in present US society and policies are aggravating vulnerability to the Asian savings glut.)

Japan in 1990 was a consensus-driven, top-down, collectivist society, economy and polity. Brian Reading, who wrote a path-breaking book called *Japan, the Coming Collapse* in 1991, called it 'not capitalism with warts, but communism with beauty spots'. Business pursued sales, not profits. Workers enjoyed the lifetime employment system, in which they were tied to employers, and benefited from firm-level pensions, health and social security, mortgages and housing, and of course salaries and bonuses. The corrupt nexus of the Liberal Democratic Party (LDP), the bureaucracy and locally based real estate interests, bound together by the tradition of Cabinet-level unanimity policed by the civil service, sorted out the spoils at both the national and local level. Business looked to Japan Inc for the direction of policy.

When the bubble burst, the various Japanese interests thought it was simply a particularly nasty cyclical experience. Businesses did not realise that future gains in output and incomes would require decision-making reoriented to profit maximisation and shareholder value, if the legacy of gross excess capacity and debt were to be worked off. This point was strengthened by the end of easy catch-up growth and the need for market forces and price signals to drive decisions once the economy was no longer simply imitating America, but operating near the technological frontier. Initially, Japanese companies cut capital spending sharply and simply waited for growth to revive. But the excess saving was structural. With business capital expenditure cut to 15% of GDP (still well above the US level, despite America's faster growth) and with housing trimmed back sharply by population slowdown, and the private savings rate edging upward from 26% to 29% of GDP, there was a chronic deficiency of demand.

The adjustment route chosen was a continuation of previous habits, without the change of behaviour that was needed. A surge of government investment projects provided the 'iron triangle' of LDP politicians, bureaucrats and local business people with huge spoils to share. And the spending was needed as a Keynesian deficit boost to demand to avoid what would probably otherwise have been a slump or depression. By 1995, interest rates had been lowered close to zero (there to remain) as the yen spiked to a peak in the low 80s against the dollar. (It quickly fell back to over 100, and has remained there ever since.) Alongside low (to zero) interest rates, the government's shift into a deficit of 5% of GDP was also crucial to sustaining demand. As the yen fell back, some growth revived into early 1997. For a while, Japanese businesses may have thought the worst was over.

At that point the government decided to claw back towards budget balance with tax increases. This was much criticised at the time, but looks correct in retrospect. As it turned out, the Asian crisis starting several months later affected Japan as well, but what was less appreciated was that even with only modest growth the economy was 3–4% overheated in spring 1997. This was because the sustainable long-run trend growth rate had fallen so far, from 5% in the 1980s to 1% in the 1990s, that only a mild growth recovery by past standards took the economy over the 'speed limit'. The time for addressing the true societal, political and supply-side issues had arrived.

Sadly, in the six or seven wasted years, as well as a much higher government debt burden, Japan's businesses had raised their debt from under six times gross operating cash flow (depreciation plus pre-interest profit) to just under seven times. The mountain to be climbed was higher and steeper. The makings of the banking crisis were in place. To get the matter in perspective, if a firm has debt of five times its gross cash flow its debt is considered junk. The US non-financial sector reached a collective ratio of 4.25–4.5 times at the post-bubble peak in mid-2001 (if official data are adjusted by adding back in off-balance-sheet debt supporting operating assets in Enron-style partnerships – much of American business's real estate, tracks, cars and trade receivables had been taken off balance sheets in this way in the 1990s). That meant perhaps one-third of the firms were above five and therefore junk. For the Japanese non-financial sector to be collectively on nearly seven times was dire. The cure was seven years of deflation.

The remainder of the story is of how Japan has remained chronically short of demand because of the violent restructuring needed to put right the acute financial conditions. In effect, Japan Inc was bust, internally, vis-à-vis its bank and household creditors; the external side showed a plenitude of overseas assets. In 2004, jobs had fallen by 0.5% a year for seven years; average pay had been carved up even more, falling 1.25% on average each year for seven years. Two recessions, in 1998 and 2001, formed part of this. The increase in business cash flow was tremendous. Its saving moved up even further than before to 25% of GDP – astonishingly nearly twice the US rate of business saving (which is itself quite strong). In cash terms, the money saved was not spent in any way but used to repay debt: this shortfall of demand was brutal debt deflation. In accounting terms, the major gains in operating profits were wiped out by provisions for depleted pension funds, losses on real estate holdings and cross-holdings of shares, much of Japanese business being plagued by old collectivist mutual ownership arrangements. By 2002 the worst was over, and the economy started a good recovery, though it was only in 2005 that labour income started to grow and house prices stabilised – probably at last presaging a boom.

What is the relevance of all this to the rest of us? In terms of the aftermath of the 1998–2000 bubble, the principal factors are the differences. But the Japanese experience gives an awful warning of the dangers of delusion and denial. Willing acceptance of much higher levels of indebtedness by governments and households has permitted a surprisingly robust growth path since 2002 in America and Britain, and 2004 in continental Europe. But the resulting burden of debt carries serious future risks, particularly when set against two other features of the financial landscape:

- **The absence of inflation.** This means that debts now have to be repaid out of real income, rather than inflated away as in 1965–95. The probable US downswing as the household borrow-and-spend game is played out and exhausted could take inflation down to very low levels, if not quite the falling prices experienced in Japan.
- **Population ageing.** The future will require the working part of the population and its capital to support much larger burdens than in the past, owing to the much increased proportion of older, retired people. Expressed in financial terms, this is like saying the obligation to pay pensions to future pensioners is a much larger propor-

tion of national income than has been true in the past. Add to this a huge pile of government and household debt inherited from battling the post-bubble torpor – or, put another way, combating excessive Asian savings – and the resources available for active members of the population could be curtailed. But of course the reduced ratio of such active people will give them greater bargaining power in offering their labour, which in normal economic logic should lead to higher, not lower, real incomes.

The result may be high real incomes for working people, but prolonged comparative poverty for the numerous old people. This could occur both directly, via inadequate resources to pay pensions, and via shrinking profit incomes as high real labour pay – plus extra taxes levied by government to finance pensioners, who would use their voting power – cuts into the flow of funds that normally goes into interest and dividend payments.

Probably the most important difference between Japan and the United States is that the US bubble did not affect real estate and house prices much. Tax cuts to stimulate US consumer spending were therefore easily reinforced by household borrowing at the Fed's much lowered short-term rates as house prices had plenty of scope to increase. In effect, while Japan had simultaneous bubbles in stocks and real estate, the United States (and Britain, Australia, Spain and even France) have been able to bring property price inflation into action as a second round of asset-price stimulus, via easy monetary policy – the 'echo-bubble' referred to earlier. Analysis of the affordability of new, higher house prices does not support the idea that they are a bubble. The much lower interest rates now prevailing are beneficial more than anything else to housing finance and land prices. The echo-bubble idea achieves its true resonance on the debt side. By 1997, Japan had a personal sector with huge net assets and low debt; but business and increasingly government were crippled with debt that took seven lean years to get back adequately towards balance. By 2005, America and Britain had business sectors with perfectly satisfactory balance sheets. But households and increasingly governments are taking on debt that could cripple the economy in future.

The Japanese experience points to the huge dangers, not on the asset side of the balance sheet but on the liability side. It is not just coincidence that Japan went through the shift into falling working-age population some ten years earlier than the West, with its baby-boomer age-group peak now, and also had its bubble ten years earlier. The debt deflation that plagued Japan when it finally faced up to its problems from 1997 onwards was also accompanied by massive provisions to restore the adequacy of pension funds, and, in a number of Japanese companies, simple arbitrary cuts in the pensions being paid – an early hint of pensioner poverty risks.

No country is more blatantly in denial about pension finance than America. As well as the issue of baby-boomers' 'inverted Alzheimer's disease', the provision for companies' pension liabilities under US accounting rules encourages their understatement for the benefit of current shareholders. Many firms are now borrowing heavily to buy back their own stock on that basis and thereby shrinking the capital base of the economy. These liabilities seriously sap the ability of the system to deal with an economic downswing, which is forecast probably for 2006, maybe later. As the burden of debt and future pensions is raised first by higher interest rates and later by demand deflation, it could keep the economy depressed for years.

6

The denouement: liquidity trap in 2006–07

The longer-term risks to America (and potentially Britain) from building up debt to 'use up' excess Asian savings are likely to be short-circuited by a cyclical downturn. What could make it worse for the United States is that the Federal Reserve's policy was reactive in the bubble and in the subsequent hard landing, and remains so now. US interest rate adjustments were 'too much, too late' in the 1998–2000 bubble, and then again in the downswing. This pattern has now been repeated in the 2003–05 upswing. In the euro zone, demand management overall was also deflationary between 2001 and 2003. Now the fiscal ease in France and Italy, combined with stimulative monetary effects there and in Spain from the common euro interest rates, is not merely 'too much, too late' but is likely to blow up the still-immature euro zone itself. To be precise, it could eventually force the weaker members to leave. America could experience a hard landing in 2006–07, and the euro zone could break up later in the decade.

In the discussion of the New Dollar Area (see Chapter 3), the sheer short-term convenience of the current set-up was raised. Americans enjoy consuming more than their output or income. China is happy to oblige with trade credit. This arrangement was not entered into voluntarily by the United States, but it has gone along with it willingly so far. Free trade has been extremely good for aggregate incomes in all countries, and for helping the poor in China and elsewhere in Asia climb up from the bottom of the income ladder. The concomitant capital gains and low interest rates have enabled even poorer Americans, whose labour has lost bargaining power, to borrow against their appreciating house prices or – for those who are not yet owners – to afford a mortgage. For better-off Americans it has been a bonanza: large rises in income associated with capital, real estate and its management; huge capital gains; and major tax cuts largely for the benefit of those on high (and relatively rising) incomes. These benign conditions are the chief reason the Bush administration easily achieved re-election in November 2004. Not unnaturally, measures to curb China's undue gains of competitiveness and to make the painful cuts in US consumption needed to reduce the external financial imbalance have been kept firmly in the realm of discussion rather than action.

This Sino-US synergy is not a formal arrangement and certainly not marriage (like EMU). It is not even agreed cohabitation. It is as if China has simply moved into the basement and taken over as servant. The danger of such arrangements was illustrated by *The Servant* (a Harold Pinter play made into a film by Joseph Losey in 1963), in which the master continued to go out into society as the man of the world, while in the home a role reversal took place:

his increasing dependence on the servant transferred true power to the latter. As long as China can dress up its own convenience to match the immediate interests of America, this process may continue. But the United States will quite soon discover the true costs of its policy, and the adjustment could be abrupt, both in domestic attitudes and in tolerance of China's mode of economic development.

There are at least three stress points in the Sino-US synergy:

- The increase of US household debt beyond viable limits, as discussed earlier.

- The loss of relative income (even absolute real income in many cases) by the poorer part of the population, whose bargaining power as labour is drastically undermined by globalisation. To illustrate the skewing of the distribution of income, consider that the average ('mean') real disposable income of the US personal sector rose in 2004 by an unusually large 5% per head. However, the median real household income fell slightly. The median is the level at which half the people have more and half have less. This combination of rising mean and falling median can only occur if relatively few incomes at the top are rising quite fast, and the majority at the bottom are falling. This is the natural result of globalisation forces within a free market economy such as America's (and few others). It has been reinforced by the Bush tax cuts, which almost exclusively favour the well-off.

- Head-on competition, rather than synergy, in demand for oil. This is not true of most energy and raw materials, for which the United States has a rapidly declining marginal appetite, but it will always be true for oil, as long as anything remotely approaching current US driving habits remains in place.

When it comes to oil, the effects are pretty concrete. China's demand for oil is 6.5 million barrels a day (mbpd) compared with over 20 mbpd for the United States and just under 50 mbpd for the OECD. But China has an 8–9% growth rate. And its oil demand tends to increase 1% for every 1% of GDP growth. So its incremental oil demand each year is over 0.5 mbpd. Other developing Asian countries (excluding Middle Eastern countries, which are mostly OPEC) have oil demand of 8.5 mbpd, reflecting the emergence of India. A similar 1-for-1 relationship of their oil demand growth to their average GDP growth of 6% means the incremental demand is the same as China's, so total incremental growth for developing Asia total is over 1 mbpd. But the OECD has only 0.4% oil demand growth for every 1% of GDP increase, because developed country growth is concentrated in service industries that use few material resources. So incremental OECD oil demand each year, given trend growth of only 2–2.5%, is a little less than 0.5 mbpd, half that of developing countries in Asia. With growing demand in other parts of the world, incremental oil demand is now some 2.25 mbpd, compared with only 1.25 mbpd as recently as ten years ago. Such is the impact of Asian emergence.

The bulk of the OECD's incremental demand is for gasoline in the United States. So the interests of American consumers are not so aligned with developing Asia's as might appear at first sight. Nor will the situation get any easier in the medium term. On the supply side, just over one-third of the world's 84–85 mbpd comes from OPEC and two-thirds from the rest of the world. But in the North Sea, output is depleting, as it is in Alaska and the other US states, and it is topping out in Canada (excluding the Athabasca tar sands) and Mexico. Russia's oil sector is being damaged by state control and crude policies (as in the 1980s), and output from other former Soviet-Union countries is hardly soaring. The rest of the world is increasing output a bit, but reliance on OPEC – which means the Gulf states, where the greater part of known reserves is located – is rising fast. To call this situation strategically lethal is an understatement.

Sino-US stress points take their toll

The hurricanes that battered America in 2005 – Katrina especially, but Rita and Wilma too – seriously exacerbated the three stress points mentioned above. With regard to oil, the cut-off of Mexican Gulf production may well be less important than the loss of 5% of US refining capacity in New Orleans. With the world short of refining capacity in any case, Katrina jerked up US gasoline prices by 20–25% in spite of European strategic reserve releases, especially by Germany. Oil's role as a stress point was sharpened.

When it comes to the distribution of income, the role of Katrina is less immediate, but probably more far-reaching. The lid was lifted from America's 'left-behinds'. This was literally true of New Orleans inhabitants fleeing the hurricane, but also metaphorically, in the sense of the whole bottom swath of

American society being left behind by globalisation and tax cuts largely concentrated on those with high incomes. The Bush administration added insult to injury by its apparently complete indifference to the emergency for a crucial few days, followed by the simple incompetence of an unqualified appointee to the relevant federal agency.

A crisis in the United States over free trade could occur at any time, when the Chinese surplus continues to grow, even explode, at the point when American consumers are hit by higher interest rates. Rebalancing of US overseas accounts, when it comes, will lead to a cut in domestic spending from 106–107% of output and incomes to something closer to 100%. In such situations people do not blame themselves, and in this case the easy target will be China. Attacks on globalisation and free trade are inevitable from opponents of the current US government, as proxies for (understandable) attacks on its tax policies.

The hurricane damage is likely to mean that monetary policy, paradoxically, will be tightened faster. Federal government spending will be the chief means of financing the rebuilding of the huge affected areas. The government's being discredited means it is likely to throw money at the problem. As it happens, shifting demand patterns of US consumer spending – not being dim, consumers are (since Katrina) buying fewer gas-guzzlers and less gasoline – are holding up the volume of spending, as people switch to buying things that are less plagued by rising prices. Meanwhile, the move back towards increasing the budget deficit means rapidly growing demand. The Fed is likely to take the view that looser fiscal policy should mean tighter monetary policy – higher interest rates sooner. So the tipping point at which household debt becomes intolerable has come closer.

The rest of the world is not standing still. The Asian surplus is redistributing itself. The handling of the huge Asian reserve build-up is also changing. In effect, the counterpart surplus to the US deficit is becoming less structural and more cyclical. It is also becoming dangerously concentrated in China, so that American anxiety about the rise of China will readily lead to political attacks when the going gets tough.

In 2004, the Eurasian structural surplus was $730 billion; this fell by nearly $200 billion to $540 billion if western Europe as a whole was included, not just the central-northern structural surplus countries centred round Germany. In 2005, the Eurasian total was estimated to have grown to $830 billion, partly because of higher Russian oil export revenues, which are cyclical, reflecting excess demand, not structural, threatening deficient demand. But the total including the whole of western Europe rather than just north-central Europe is only up to $575 billion, as deficits have grown fast in Mediterranean Europe. Meanwhile, as well as oil revenue gains boosting Russia's surplus, the surplus of other oil exporters (including OPEC) was expected to increase by $100 billion in 2005 to $150 billion. So there are two phenomena:

- Within Europe, imbalances are increasing between the sustained north-central surplus and the growing deficits in the Mediterranean region.
- Treating western Europe as a whole, the world is seeing a roughly sustained level of structural surplus – now properly called the Asian,

rather than Eurasian, savings glut – with a much increased overall imbalance owing to oil exporters' gains (and growing deficits, chiefly in America).

Concerning the lower US bond yields resulting from the Asian savings excess, Tim Congdon, a celebrated British economist and former colleague, recently asked: 'What happens when the surpluses go away?' That will no doubt happen at some stage, but not yet. However, a cyclical, oil-producer surplus is a symptom of excess demand: exactly the opposite of the structural Asian surplus. Unlike the structural surpluses that reflect a deficiency of demand, these surpluses arise from Sino-US competition for oil. Increasingly, oil-exporters' surpluses will further increase demand as they spend the money on imports. The shift of surpluses towards this cyclical element may imply higher bond yields.

It is impressive that the structural surplus in north-central Europe – Germany, Benelux, Scandinavia, Switzerland and Austria – is little changed, despite higher oil prices. Germany's quintuple deflation (exchange rate, fiscal, monetary, restructuring and demographic) has created such rapidly increasing competitiveness that it offsets extra oil costs. But these exports are to a large degree at the expense of Italy, Spain, Portugal and Greece, where rapid demand growth nurtures lower-cost, central-northern European exporters, who are gaining market share. The EU's balance of payments overall, including Britain, which runs a deficit, and the recent east-central EU entrants, shifted by $100 billion at an annual rate between early and late 2005. Of this huge change, about half reflects higher oil costs and the rest real increases of imports ahead of exports. So the Eurasian savings excess we have spoken of has become Ben Bernanke's 'Asian savings glut'.

The expansion of demand in Europe, and the resulting fall in its overall surplus, takes it out of the global argument over financial imbalances. But within the euro zone the imbalances are rapidly increasing. It is one thing for German labour-cost deflation to eliminate its overvaluation at the inception of EMU in 1999. It is quite another for Italian and Spanish costs now to continue growing by 3% or so faster than Germany's. The effect is that lack of export competitiveness forces Italy and Spain to rely increasingly on domestic demand for growth, with rapidly increasing trade deficits. Certainly in Italy already, and probably in Spain once the current hectic real estate boom lapses, this domestic demand growth requires growing government deficits. In Italy, government debt is already over 100% of GDP. The permanently fixed exchange rates between EMU countries (its chief feature) mean these imbalances can be expected to grow, unless the Mediterranean countries at some point engage in drastic deflation. It is unlikely that they will do so as readily as Germany in 2001–04. So the current mechanism of euro-zone growth will probably require at least Italy to fall out of EMU within a few years. (For Spain, Portugal and Greece, the issue is less clear, as faster labour-cost growth may be offset by them starting from a much lower level, unlike Italy.)

Meanwhile in Japan, domestic demand is growing. Labour income is finally increasing, after falling for seven years, and household confidence is further boosted by the end of major house-

Table 2 **China's exploding current-account surplus***

	2004	2005	2006	2007	2008	2009	2010
$ billion							
Exports	593	771	964	1,205	1,507	1,883	2,354
Slow imports	561	656	787	945	1,134	1,360	1,632
Fast imports	561	656	820	1,025	1,281	1,602	2,002
Invisibles	35	35	35	35	35	35	35
Current-account balance ($ billion)							
Slow imports	**68**	**151**	**212**	**296**	**408**	**558**	**757**
Fast imports	**68**	**151**	**180**	**216**	**261**	**317**	**388**
Annual growth (%)							
Exports	–	30	25	25	25	25	25
Imports (slow)	–	17	20	20	20	20	20
Imports (fast)	–	17	25	25	25	25	25

*as published early 2006: estimated for 2005 and forecast for 2006–10

price deflation. The surplus is little changed, as growing imports and higher oil costs are offset by buoyant exports, stimulated by the global boom, especially in America. Among the Asian Tigers, there is a more muted revival of domestic demand, and a greater impact of the slowdown of exports to China (their most important market) as well as the impact of oil prices. For China and the Tigers, the increase of oil prices in 2005 cost about 3% of GDP (from 5% to 8%). In China's case this effect is dampened in the short term by price controls and domestic production (also price-controlled) of about 40% of its demand. For other Tigers, such price controls as exist are less benign, severely affecting industrial behaviour as well as consumer thrift in response to world shortage. So Asian Tiger surpluses are reducing somewhat.

China's surplus, however, is exploding, despite higher oil import costs. Exports continued to rise at more than 30% in 2005 (only temporarily held back by the so-called EU 'bra wars'). But imports are up by only 15–17%, including the effect of higher oil prices. This could raise the current surplus from 2004's $70 billion by some $80 billion in 2005 to $150 billion (over 8% of GDP). Without higher oil prices 2005's surplus would approach $200 billion. On modest assumptions for the future, China's surplus will rise to $400 billion by 2010. It does not take extravagant assumptions to get that projection to twice that level, which would be a quarter of 2010's probable GDP. This would not be tolerated. And we know who will be first not to tolerate it. Although Europe has a less strong politico-intellectual tradition in favour of free trade than the United States, it has no serious mechanism for sustained obstruction of imports, outside the Common Agricultural Policy (which mostly hits African countries, not fast-growth Asia). But the US Congress has already voted for a huge tariff on Chinese imports and will probably soon revive the proposal if and when the pain level increases.

This rapid shift of the Asian surplus to China is no surprise, given its leading role in ensuring excessive Asian competitiveness via the yuan–dollar peg. But it helps take the focus off the US deficit and place it squarely on China's surplus, rather than some diffuse Eurasian structural problem. Meanwhile, the other increases in surplus counterparts to the US deficit are cyclical: much greater OPEC and Russian/former-Soviet-Union surpluses. The latter will dissipate over time. Either oil prices will fall, or these countries' imports will rise. So the cyclical forces are in favour of excess demand. In 2005, only China had slower domestic demand growth. Demand is accelerating in Europe, Japan, the Asian Tigers (mildly) and oil exporters. It is also accelerating in the United States, where unabated capital gains are ensuring capital-gains-related income growth as well as rampant household credit growth, at the same time as the federal government is borrowing to finance post-hurricane rebuilding.

Mercantilist China: exchange-rate policy on the defensive

China's 2% revaluation of the yuan in July 2005, from 8.28/$ to 8.11/$, was the first, badly executed step down a long road. The explosion of the Chinese surplus had already put close observers – most obviously Asian central banks – on notice that the yuan would have to appreciate mightily in the relatively near term. China's half-baked blunder told them it would be done reluctantly, defensively and incompetently. At this stage, given the excessive domestic boom of 2003–04 resulting from China's mercantilist exchange-rate policy, no reasonable shift in the yuan will do much to slow the growth of exports. The marginal labour cost of exports is small, once industrial capacity has been installed (excessive capacity in the Chinese case). Labour costs are especially small in China, which is why so much capacity has been installed there. If the exchange rate is raised by 25%, say, the extra yuan cost of labour will still leave it profitable at the margin to export. The revenue from exports will still greatly exceed their marginal cost, since a large part of the total cost is the sunk cost of the original capital investment. This is particularly true in energy and materials-intensive China, where the yuan cost of dollar-priced imported energy and materials will become lower after an appreciation of the yuan. So even the marginal costs of production are in many cases diminished by currency appreciation.

The combination of continued rapid Chinese surplus growth under almost any exchange-rate scenario is likely to prove a red rag to the US congressional bull. With the president's authority much reduced, and congressional elections looming at the end of 2006, the first of the three stress points in the Sino-US synergy to be tested could be the damage from globalisation to the American poor. The growing Chinese surplus is a monthly reminder of the pressure on their jobs and incomes. American politicians in general do not make the link between globalisation and the Asian surpluses on the one hand, and the capital gains and cheap debt enjoyed by most Americans on the other. They ascribe these mostly to their own merits, and largely focus on the downside of Asian economic emergence. After Katrina, and given the obscurity of China's policymaking and the defensive incompetence of its exchange-rate management, the public argument in America is dominated by aggressive anti-Chinese rhetoric. So far, fairly moderate textile trade restrictions are all that have resulted, but much worse is quite likely. Even these restrictions, by inhibiting freedom of supply, are clearly inflationary in implication.

The other two stress points in Sino-US synergy are energy and raw material prices, and US household debt. Both are affected by the increasing breadth and strength of the world boom. Taking energy first, the upward pressure on prices has to remain strong until US growth is clearly slowing. To be sure, the upward spike of oil and refined product prices after Katrina has been duly reversed, but the forces behind rising prices have not gone away. This is not just a matter of the medium-term demand growth and supply constraints discussed earlier. It is also true in the short-term cyclical sense, as long as US growth continues. European and Japanese growth is not the problem. But China's domestic demand and GDP slowdown from early 2004 to early 2005 is being temporarily reversed by the sheer force of its export growth. China's oil demand in early 2005 was actually down from early 2004, as slower growth was reinforced by working off oil inventory built up in 2003–04. Its oil demand could now pick up as growth continues. Only a US downswing would slow the exports that are China's mainspring, but US growth is accelerating. The Chinese benefit from this knocks on to the oil-intensive Tigers too. Upward pressure on oil prices should soon reassert itself.

The US expansion is now broadly based and no longer largely dependent on household spending stimulated by tax cuts and low interest rates. Business capital spending has steady momentum, growing at high single-figure rates, as is housing. As well as consumers continuing to spend, the government has to respond to rebuilding needs in areas ravaged by hurricanes. Businesses cut inventories in mid-2005 but are now likely to build them up again to supply growing demand. On top of all this, the recovering demand of Europe and Japan is stimulating exports, aided by the US cost benefits of three years of dollar devaluation. As a result, in volume terms, for all the trade deficit problems with China, US exports are outstripping imports for the first time in years, resulting in a gain in net exports. For the past few years, negative net exports have cut 0.5–0.75% a year from domestic demand – this is part of the Sino-US synergy by which demand increases without inflationary pressure. Now, in a major switch, net exports may be adding some 0.5%.

Ironically, it is the removal of worsening US trade volumes that most threatens an economic hard landing in the near term, as opposed to a crippling long-run debt build-up if recent imbalances were to persist. Added to the pressure of domestic demand already growing at more than 4%, about 1% above the 'speed limit' (the 3% long-run sustainable potential growth rate), it means growth could accelerate towards 5%. The Fed is likely to be raising short-term US interest rates until well into 2006. They could reach 5% by the summer of 2006. In addition, the upswing in Europe and Japan, meaning much broader demand growth globally than when it was concentrated in America and Britain, is putting upward pressure on longer-term rates and bond yields.

US household debt: the weak link in 2006–07

This highlights the most important of the three stress points in Sino-US synergy: the potentially ruinous build-up of US household debt it entails. Much higher debt burdens give the Fed a significantly harder task in slowing the economy. At the moment, apart from exports (which remain relatively small at little over

10% of GDP), US growth depends ultimately on capital gains. These account for more than half the growth of labour income (via stock option exercise, real estate commissions, bonuses, and the like). They also underpin the willingness to borrow – and it is only by US households raising their real debt burden by 10% a year that consumer demand is kept from falling back relative to income. In other words, as well as providing half the growth of labour income, capital gains are essential to the net savings rate staying at zero – without which consumer spending would fall short of income. But at some stage the rise in interest rates and bond yields is likely to have two interactive effects. It will:

- reduce the affordability of housing loans, thereby curbing credit growth;
- reduce buyers' willingness to pay higher house prices.

But lower capital gains will mean the capital-related part of labour income – stock option gains, real estate commissions and bonuses – falls rather than rises. At that point total labour income growth will be less than conventional payrolls, normal pay excluding stock options, and so on. However, conventional payrolls are growing at only 3%. As and when that becomes the ceiling for total labour income growth, real labour incomes will have stopped growing, given inflation of 2–3%. That is exactly the stage at which household debt will start to feel burdensome, with income growth falling and interest costs rising. Housing afford-ability by then will be distinctly less. So the savings rate will rise just at the point that income is slowing. This double whammy is what the Fed rightly fears when it talks of deflationary risks being greater than inflationary ones. It is right, but the situation is not under control. The mode of expansion of the United States in the past three years, becoming dependent on vendor financing from Asia, has made this type of hard landing ineluctable.

A mitigating factor is that better European and Japanese growth should help export demand and soften the rebalancing away from 6–7% deficits. But there is an iron logic to this, too. US GDP is at or rather above its 'potential', i.e. a touch overheated. There is no scope for permitting net export rebalancing without cutting the ratio of domestic demand to GDP (i.e. income), which is now 106–107%. GDP is already above potential so extra GDP growth is not an escape route. It is domestic demand that has to adjust downwards. Exports may grow, holding up employment, but in that case real disposable income, and real spending per head, must be cut. In the absence of tax increases to reduce spending power, this can probably be achieved only by a major cyclical downswing – led by much reduced real income related to capital gains – and by sharp cuts in credit to households. The monetary policy process was described in the previous paragraph.

This snapping shut of the Asian glut liquidity trap is likely to be soon, in late 2006 or 2007. But US households have not been prepared for the idea that they cannot consume 6–7% more than they produce. It is regarded as an entitlement. Those at the lower end of the income scale will look around for someone to blame, and, as seen in past and present Democratic Party rhetoric, it will be China and/or globalisation, a.k.a. 'outsourcing'. In fact, large US income gains have been made possible by free importation of cheap goods from Asia. Any attempt to restrict imports will increase average costs and decrease average real incomes, making the drop in living standards that much more severe. But the switch to a US downswing will probably occur against the provocative backdrop of a soaring Chinese export surplus. At best, the result will be a huge yuan revaluation with substantial upward moves of the yen and the euro. In that case US exports would do well, and adjustment could be quite rapid, provided that either taxes were raised or monetary tightness was maintained. Political unpopularity is inevitable under any likely scenario. But the danger is that the US commitment to free trade and globalisation proves shallow. In that case a much deeper crisis will ensue.

As always in making gloomy predictions, the question must be confronted: supposing they are wrong. If the structural surplus does not shrink quite rapidly, growth might be maintained for several years on the recent pattern, with Asia continuing to underwrite cheap US and European borrowing. This is the 'denial' option, with likely consequences similar to Japan's (see Chapter 5). Essentially, the build-up of western debt to Asia will collide with the crystallisation of the baby-boomers' pension problem – those born in 1946 reaching 65 in 2011. The problem boils down to an almost Socratic dilemma: either the Asian surplus is sharply reduced quite soon, or it is not. If it is, the United States must accept a major income cut in the next couple of years, almost certainly involving a hard landing or recession. If it is not, growth will be blighted for years from 2009–10, and the baby-boomers' poverty trap will become a reality.

Notes

1 Lombard Street Research's *Monthly International Review (MIR)* no. 143, September 2004: 'US balance sheets serially trashed by Eurasian surplus', Charles Dumas. Dr Bernanke's speech was given on 10 March 2005.

2 Lombard Street Research's *MIR* no. 122, November 2002: 'Emerging Eurasia to dominate world economy by 2025', Charles Dumas.

3 Lombard Street Research's *MIR* no. 97, July 2000: 'US corporate profits: sharp fall likely in 2001–02. E-dementia misallocates resources – www hitting USA.com and USA Inc', Charles Dumas.

4 See note 2.

Index